Celebrity Chefs

More Than 60 Delicious Recipes

Bobby Flay's 16-Spice Fried Chicken
with Mango–Red Chile Honey (recipe on page 84)

Celebrity Chefs

More Than 60 Delicious Recipes

HEARST BOOKS
New York

Bobby Flay's
Red Curry-Marinated
Skirt Steak Fajitas
(recipe on page 110)

Contents

Meet the Chefs

Everyone loves and appreciates a good meal and your favorite famous chefs are no different. This cookbook gathers recipes from some of the best chefs in the world, with Bobby Flay, Marcus Samuelsson, Martha Stewart, Emeril Lagasse, and Rocco DiSpirito sharing pages with Sara Moulton, Deborah Madison, Todd English, Mark Bittman, Alice Waters, and many more. Get ready to prepare a star-studded meal!

Ted Allen

Ted Allen is host of Food Network's *Chopped*, winner of two James Beard Awards—one for the show itself, the other for Ted as host—and is a contributor on Food Network's *The Best Thing I Ever Ate*.

Previously a judge on Bravo's *Top Chef* and Food Network's *Iron Chef America*, Ted was the food and wine specialist on Bravo's Emmy-winning *Queer Eye*. He wrote *In My Kitchen*; *The Food You Want to Eat*; and co-authored *Queer Eye for the Straight Guy*.

A contributing writer for *Esquire* since 1997, Ted also writes for such publications as *Bon Appétit* and *Food Network Magazine*.

Lidia Bastianich

One of the best-loved chefs on television, a best-selling cookbook author, cookware designer, and restaurateur, **Lidia Bastianich** has married her two passions in life—family and food.

Her cookbooks include *Lidia's Favorite Recipes* and *Lidia's Italy*—companion books to the award-winning television series, *Lidia's Italy in America* and *Lidia's Italy*. Owners of four acclaimed New York City restaurants, as well as Lidia's Pittsburgh and Lidia's Kansas City, she and her son, Joseph, are also part owners of Eataly, the largest artisanal Italian food and wine marketplace in New York City. With her daughter, Tanya, she designed the Lidia's Kitchen line of cookware for QVC.

Rick Bayless

Winner of several James Beard Awards and Bravo's Top Chef Master, **Rick Bayless** is also the host of the highly rated public television series *Mexico—One Plate at a Time*. He has authored eight award-winning cookbooks and runs his side-by-side award-winning Chicago restaurants, Frontera Grill and Topolobampo, both founded in 1987. His Frontera line of salsas, grilling sauces, and organic chips can be found from coast to coast.

Beekman Boys
(Brent Ridge & Josh Kilmer-Purcell)

When **Josh Kilmer-Purcell** and **Dr. Brent Ridge** bought the Beekman Farm in upstate New York in 2008, they didn't just start a farm, they started a movement. Now they have a hit TV show, best-selling books, product lines, and a James Beard–nominated lifestyle website.

Known as *The Fabulous Beekman Boys* from their reality show on Cooking Channel, they are authors of *The Beekman 1802 Heirloom Cookbook* and a memoir of their farm life, *The Bucolic Plague*. In 2012, millions watched as they went from "ultimate underdogs" to first-place winners on CBS's *The Amazing Race*.

John Besh

New Orleans native son **John Besh** is dedicated to the culinary riches of southern Louisiana. In 1999, *Food & Wine* named him one of the "Top 10 Best New Chefs in America," and he won the James Beard Award for "Best Chef: Southeast" in 2006. He owns nine acclaimed restaurants; his flagship, August, is a Gayot Top 40 Restaurant, a Wine Enthusiast Top 100 Restaurant, and a 2012 nominee for the James Beard "Best National Restaurant" award.

A frequent guest on NBC's *Today* show, Besh has authored two IACP Award–winning cookbooks, *My New Orleans* and *My Family Table*. He hosts two television cooking shows, *Chef John Besh's New Orleans* and *Chef John Besh's Family Table*.

Mark Bittman

Mark Bittman, whose "Minimalist" column ran in the Dining section of *The New York Times* for more than 13 years, is a *Times* Opinion columnist, the lead food writer for *The New York Times Magazine*, and a columnist for the *Times* Dining section. His books include the bestselling *How to Cook Everything*, the groundbreaking *Food Matters*, and his latest offering, *VB6*, about his diet of eating only vegan food before 6:00 p.m.

Rocco DiSpirito

Rocco DiSpirito was working in the kitchens of legendary chefs by age twenty. He was named *Food & Wine*'s "Best New Chef" in 1999 and was the first chef to win *Gourmet*'s "America's Most Exciting Young Chef." His restaurant Union Pacific was a New York City culinary landmark and he now runs the Now Eat This! Truck, whose proceeds provide free, healthy lunches to New York City students.

He is also the author of nine books, including the *New York Times* best sellers *Now Eat This!*, *Now Eat This! Diet*, and, most recently, *Now Eat This! Italian*.

He hosts the syndicated television show *Now Eat This! with Rocco DiSpirito*.

Ree Drummond

Ree Drummond is the #1 *New York Times* best-selling author of *The Pioneer Woman Cooks: Recipes from an Accidental Country Girl* and *The Pioneer Woman Cooks: Food from My Frontier*. Her beloved website, The Pioneer Woman, was founded in 2006 and showcases her cooking, photography, and anecdotes about country life. Her cooking show, *The Pioneer Woman*, premiered on Food Network in 2011. Ree lives on a working cattle ranch in Oklahoma with her husband and four children.

Todd English

Four-time James Beard Award–winner **Todd English** is a renowned chef, restaurateur, author, entrepreneur, and television star. He has established Olives as one of the most prestigious restaurant names in the nation with multiple locations, and he also owns several other restaurants, including the Todd English Food Hall at the Plaza Hotel in New York City. He has authored four critically acclaimed cookbooks, has created a record-breaking housewares line, the Todd English Collection, and currently hosts an Emmy-nominated PBS travel series, *Food Trip with Todd English*.

Lisa Fain

A seventh-generation Texan currently residing in New York City, **Lisa Fain** writes and photographs the award-winning food blog Homesick Texan. She is also the author of *The Homesick Texan Cookbook*, which was an IACP finalist for best American cookbook, a 2011 *New York Times* notable cookbook, and named one of the top ten cookbooks of 2011 by *The Washington Post*, Epicurious.com, and Amazon.com, among others. She is also a certified barbecue judge.

Guy Fieri

In 2006, **Guy Fieri** premiered his first show, *Guy's Big Bite*, on Food Network. Today, he hosts *Diners, Drive-Ins and Dives*, and guest judges on *Food Network Star*. Guy collaborates with Rachael Ray in the competition series *Rachael vs. Guy Celebrity Cook-Off*.

Along with Steve Gruber, Guy owns multiple locations of Johnny Garlic's and Tex Wasabi's, their California-based restaurants.

Guy's books include *Diners, Drive-Ins and Dives; More Diners, Drive-Ins and Dives*; and *Guy Fieri Food*.

Bobby Flay

Owner of several much-loved restaurants, including Mesa Grill, Bar Americain, Bobby Flay Steak, and Bobby's Burger Palace, **Bobby Flay** also shares his knowledge and enthusiasm for food through his cookbooks and cooking programs. His eleventh cookbook, *Bobby Flay's Bar Americain Cookbook*, hit bookstores in 2011.

He shares his culinary talents and passions with television viewers every day, currently starring in *Iron Chef America*, *Throwdown! with Bobby Flay*, *Grill It! with Bobby Flay* (the 2009 Emmy Award winner for Outstanding Culinary Program), *Bobby Flay's Barbecue Addiction* (the 2012 Emmy Award winner for Outstanding Culinary Program), and *Brunch @ Bobby's* on Cooking Channel.

Sara Foster

Sara Foster is one of the country's foremost experts on simple food prepared with local and seasonal ingredients. After years of success in catering, in 1990 she opened Foster's Market, an award-winning gourmet market café in Durham, NC, followed by a second location in Chapel Hill.

She is the author of two cookbooks, *The Foster's Market Cookbook* and *Fresh Every Day: More Great Recipes from Foster's Market*, and was the contributing food editor for *Cottage Living*.

Amanda Freitag

One of New York City's most celebrated chefs, **Amanda Freitag** is the former executive chef of The Harrison and has worked under the notable tutelage of Jean-Georges Vongerichten and Tom Valenti.

She has battled Bobby Flay on *Iron Chef America* and frequently serves as a judge on the Food Network series *Chopped*. She is currently a contributing chef on Cooking Channel's *Unique Eats*.

Gregory Gourdet

Gregory Gourdet creates approachable, modern Asian cuisine using both traditional and avant-garde techniques. He attended the Culinary Institute of America and later became chef de cuisine of 66, a former Jean-Georges modern Chinese restaurant.

He is now chef de cuisine of Departures in Portland, OR. In 2012, he won the Great American Seafood Cook-Off in New Orleans, becoming the first chef outside of a Gulf state to win this esteemed contest.

David Guas

A New Orleans native, **David Guas** worked as a corporate pastry chef for ten years before opening Bayou Bakery, Coffee Bar & Eatery in Arlington, VA. His cookbook *DamGoodSweet: Desserts to Satisfy Your Sweet Tooth New Orleans Style* was named one of *Food & Wine*'s "Best New Dessert Cookbooks" of 2009; it was also nominated for a James Beard Award in the Baking and Dessert Cookbook category.

Carla Hall

A co-host on ABC's *The Chew*, **Carla Hall** is the owner of Alchemy by Carla Hall, an artisan cookie company. A native of Nashville, she worked as a sous chef at the Henley Park Hotel and as executive chef at the State Plaza Hotel and the Washington Club, and has taught classes at CulinAerie and her alma mater, L'Academie de Cuisine. Hall lives in Washington, DC, and New York with her husband, Matthew Lyons, and stepson, Noah.

Stephanie Izard

Winner of Bravo's *Top Chef: Season Four*, **Stephanie Izard** is the executive chef of the Chicago restaurants Girl & the Goat and Little Goat. She was nominated for the James Beard Foundation's "Best Chef: Great Lakes" award in 2012, while Girl & the Goat was nominated for "Best New Restaurant" in 2011. Named one of *Food & Wine*'s "Best New Chefs" of 2011, Stephanie published her first book, *Girl in the Kitchen*, that same year.

She has worked in some of the most respected kitchens in Chicago, including La Tache, Spring, and Vong, as well as her own highly acclaimed restaurant, Scylla.

Hubert Keller

A Frenchman classically trained by France's top chefs, **Hubert Keller** owns the world-renowned restaurants Fleur de Lys San Francisco and Fleur by Hubert Keller in Las Vegas, as well as the popular Burger Bar restaurants in Las Vegas, St. Louis, and San Francisco. He has won numerous awards, including the James Beard Foundation's "Best Chef: California."

In 2009, Keller was a contestant on Bravo's *Top Chef Masters*. He also hosts a cooking show on PBS, *Secrets of a Chef*, now entering its fourth season. His cookbook, *Hubert Keller's Souvenirs: Stories & Recipes From My Life*, was released in 2012.

Emeril Lagasse

Emeril Lagasse is the chef/proprietor of thirteen restaurants in New Orleans; Las Vegas; Orlando; Bethlehem, PA; and Charlotte, NC. As a national TV personality, he has hosted more than 2,000 shows on Food Network and is the food correspondent for ABC's *Good Morning America*. Most recently, Emeril joined *Top Chef Seattle* as the show's newest addition to the judges' table. His latest show, *Emeril's Florida*, premiered in 2013 on Cooking Channel. Emeril is the best-selling author of seventeen cookbooks, including his latest, *Emeril's Kicked-Up Sandwiches*.

Nigella Lawson

Food enthusiast, television personality, and journalist, **Nigella Lawson** is the author of eight best-selling books, including *Nigella Kitchen*, *Nigella Fresh*, *Nigella Christmas*, *Nigella Bites*, *Feast*, *How to Be a Domestic Goddess*, and *How to Eat*, which have sold more than 6 million copies worldwide. Her books, ground-breaking iPhone app, and television shows on Food Network, E! Entertainment Television, and Style Network have made her a global household name. She currently hosts a new culinary competition series, *The Taste*, on ABC, with Anthony Bourdain, Ludo Lefebvre, and Brian Malarkey.

Katie Lee

Writer and host **Katie Lee** wrote *The Comfort Table* and *The Comfort Table: Recipes for Everyday Occasions* cookbooks.

She was the host of season one of Bravo's *Top Chef*, has served as a food and lifestyle contributor for *The Early Show*, and appeared on *Oprah*, *Today*, *The Rachael Ray Show*, and *Iron Chef America*. She writes a column for *Self*, and her recipes have appeared in *People*, *Cosmopolitan*, *Food & Wine*, and *Town & Country*.

Sandra Lee

Sandra Lee is an Emmy Award winner and internationally acclaimed expert in all things kitchen and home.

She is the editor in chief of *Sandra Lee Magazine* and the host of four highly rated culinary programs on Food Network and Cooking Channel: *Restaurant Remakes*, *Sandra's Money Saving Meals*, *Semi-Homemade Cooking*, and *Taverns, Lounges & Clubs*. Sandra has launched several lines of home, garden, seasonal, and craft products and produced a successful DIY home-improvement series.

In spring 2013, this *New York Times* best-selling author of twenty-five cookbooks released her newest cooking title, *Every Dish Delivers*. Her first novel, *The Recipe Box*, is due July 2013.

Deborah Madison

The founding chef of Greens restaurant in San Francisco, **Deborah Madison** is also the author of innumerable articles on food and farming as well as twelve cookbooks, including *Vegetarian Cooking for Everyone*, *Local Flavors*, *What We Eat When We Eat Alone*, and, most recently, *Vegetable Literacy*. Two of her books were named Cookbook of the Year by the IACP and she has won several James Beard Awards.

Daisy Martinez

A Brooklyn, New York, native born to Puerto Rican parents, **Daisy Martinez** attended the French Culinary Institute in 1998.

The star of PBS's *Daisy Cooks!* and Food Network's *Viva Daisy!*, she is the author of several cookbooks, including *Daisy Cooks! Latin Flavors that Will Rock Your World*, winner of the Best Latino Cuisine Cookbook by the Gourmand World Cookbook Awards. She is also a columnist for *Every Day with Rachael Ray* and *Selecciones* magazines.

Sara Moulton

As a protégée of Julia Child, founder of the New York Women's Culinary Alliance, executive chef of *Gourmet* magazine, food editor of ABC's *Good Morning America*, and the host of several popular shows on Food Network during that channel's first decade, **Sara Moulton** has made her mark again and again.

She is the author of several cookbooks, including *Sara's Secrets for Weeknight Meals* and *Sara Moulton's Everyday Family Dinners*. In 2011, she launched "Sara's Kitchen," an iPhone app featuring sixty recipes. This year marks her third season as host of public television's *Sara's Weeknight Meals*.

Wolfgang Puck

The name **Wolfgang Puck** is synonymous with the best of restaurant hospitality and the ultimate in all aspects of the culinary arts. With dozens of restaurants across the country—including his revered Spago in Los Angeles—six cookbooks, and countless houseware and food products carrying his renowned brand name, he has built a multifaceted culinary empire. His Emmy Award–winning television series, *Wolfgang Puck*, debuted on Food Network in 2000 and aired for five seasons. With regular appearances on ABC's *Good Morning America* and on Home Shopping Network, as well as guest appearances on a wide variety of programs over the last two decades, Wolfgang Puck is known to millions around the world.

Rachael Ray

Rachael Ray got her start in upstate New York as the manager of the famed Sagamore Resort. When her cooking classes attracted the attention of the local CBS affiliate, she began filming a weekly segment called *30-Minute Meals* for the evening news.

Her television work evolved into several Food Network shows, including *Tasty Travels*, *$40 a Day*, and *30-Minute Meals*, which won a Daytime Emmy Award in 2006. That year, she launched her award-winning syndicated series *Rachael Ray*. Her newest show is Cooking Channel's *Rachael Ray's Week in a Day*.

She is the author of dozens of successful cookbooks, and also runs the lifestyle magazine *Everyday with Rachael Ray*.

Marcus Samuelsson

Marcus Samuelsson is an internationally acclaimed chef, philanthropist, and *New York Times* best-selling author. He has been honored by the James Beard Foundation on multiple occasions, garnering the "Rising Star Chef" award in 1999, the "Best Chef: New York City" award in 2003, and the "Best International Cookbook" award in 2007. He won the second season of Bravo's *Top Chef Masters* and was crowned *Chopped: All Stars* champion in 2012.

In 2010, Samuelsson opened the Red Rooster Harlem restaurant, and in 2012, he and Andrew Chapman opened Ginny's Supper Club, both in New York City.

Steven Satterfield

During his twenty years in restaurants, **Steven Satterfield** has developed strong relationships with local farmers—a connection that is integral to his and co-owner Neal McCarthy's exciting restaurant venture, Miller Union in Atlanta.

In 2011, he was nominated for *Food & Wine*'s "People's Best New Chef." Miller Union earned a spot on the Best New Restaurants in America lists from *Bon Appétit* and *Esquire*, as well as *Atlanta* magazine's Restaurant of the Year in 2010.

Barton Seaver

A recognized leader in the sustainable seafood movement, **Barton Seaver** was also a fellow with the Blue Oceans Institute and is currently a fellow with the National Geographic Society.

Named the 2009 "Chef of the Year" by *Esquire* magazine, he has manned the helm of many popular restaurants in Washington, DC, and is the host of the television series *In Search of Food* on Ovation Network, as well as a National Geographic web video series called *CookWise*. He is the author of two cookbooks, *For Cod and Country: Simple, Delicious, Sustainable Cooking* and *Where There's Smoke: Simple, Sustainable, Delicious Grilling*.

Martha Stewart

Entrepreneur, Emmy Award–winning TV show host, and founder of Martha Stewart Living Omnimedia, **Martha Stewart** is the author of numerous best-selling cookbooks, including *Martha Stewart's Cooking School*, which is also a PBS series.

A former caterer whose elegant recipes and unique visual presentation of food became a cornerstone of the company she founded in 1996, she is America's most trusted lifestyle expert and teacher. Her namesake company reaches approximately 66 million consumers across all media platforms each month. The company also offers a range of products in such retail locations as Home Depot, Macy's, Staples, PetSmart, Michaels, Jo-Ann Fabric & Craft Stores, and jcpenney.

Christina Tosi

Christina Tosi is the chef, owner, and founder of Momofuku Milk Bar, called "one of the most exciting bakeries in the country" by *Bon Appétit*. As founder of the dessert program at Momofuku restaurants, she helped Momofuku Ko earn two stars from the Michelin Guide and Momofuku Ssäm jump onto *Restaurant* magazine's list of the top 100 restaurants in the world. She is the 2012 recipient of the James Beard "Rising Star Chef" award. She lives in Brooklyn with her three dogs and eats an unconscionable amount of raw cookie dough every day.

Ming Tsai

James Beard Award–winning chef and owner of Blue Ginger and Blue Dragon, both in Massachusetts, **Ming Tsai** is an Emmy Award–winning host of PBS's *Simply Ming*, now in its tenth season. He is the author of five cookbooks: *Blue Ginger: East Meets West Cooking with Ming Tsai, Simply Ming, Ming's Master Recipes, Simply Ming One-Pot Meals*, and his latest, *Simply Ming in Your Kitchen*. For more information on Ming, visit www.ming.com.

Alice Waters

Owner of Chez Panisse Restaurant in Berkeley, CA, **Alice Waters** has championed local, sustainable farms for over four decades. She is the founder of the Edible Schoolyard at Berkeley's Martin Luther King Jr. Middle School, a model public-education program that integrates edible education into the core curriculum, with hands-on planting, harvesting, and cooking. The mission of her nonprofit organization, the Edible Schoolyard Project, is to gather and share the lessons and best practices of school gardens, kitchens, and edible education programs worldwide.

She is also the author of ten books, including *40 Years of Chez Panisse: The Power of Gathering* and *The Edible Schoolyard: A Universal Idea*.

Gregory Gourdet's Escarole-Chicken Dumplings (recipe on page 35)

Appetizers

Start your meal with a bang by cooking up a few of these delicious and creative recipes from some of your favorite chefs. Emeril Lagasse's Herbed Goat Cheese Buttons and Hubert Keller's Mango-Avocado Bruschetta are the perfect party foods to get your guests in a festive mood.

Emeril Lagasse's
Herbed Goat Cheese Buttons

Total time 23 minutes plus chilling

Makes 14 buttons

11 oz. goat cheese, softened	½ tsp. finely chopped fresh rosemary or thyme leaves	⅛ tsp. freshly ground black pepper, plus more to taste
2 Tbsp. finely chopped fresh basil leaves	1 to 2 Tbsp. extra-virgin olive oil, plus more for serving	Fresh herb sprigs, for garnish (optional)
1 Tbsp. finely chopped fresh oregano leaves	¼ tsp. kosher salt, plus more to taste	
1½ tsp. finely chopped garlic		

1 In a small bowl, combine goat cheese, basil, oregano, garlic, rosemary, and 1 tablespoon oil; stir until well combined. If mixture is too stiff to mix well, gradually add remaining oil as necessary, and stir to combine. Stir in salt and freshly ground black pepper. Cover and refrigerate 30 minutes to 1 hour or until stiffened.

2 With a small spoon, in roughly 2-tablespoon portions, scoop cheese mixture onto sheet of waxed paper. With lightly oiled hands, roll each portion into a ball, then flatten slightly to form a "button." Line platter with herb sprigs, if you like. Place buttons on platter; cover with plastic wrap and refrigerate up to 1 day. To serve, allow buttons to come to room temperature. Drizzle with oil.

Each button About 95 calories, 5 g protein, 1 g carbohydrate, 8 g total fat (5 g saturated), 0 g fiber, 18 mg cholesterol, 155 mg sodium.

Emeril loves using these goat cheese buttons to spice up a dinner party:
"These are a wonderful spread for crackers or crusty bread, and they make a nice addition to a cheese plate or a simple green salad."

Beekman Boys'
Deviled Eggs with Smoked Trout

Total time 35 minutes

Makes 8 servings

8 large eggs
⅓ c. half-and-half
2 Tbsp. mayonnaise
1 tsp. Dijon mustard

½ tsp. medium-hot curry powder
½ tsp. salt
4 oz. smoked trout, torn into small bits

2 Tbsp. plus 1 tsp. fresh lemon juice
¼ c. minced scallions

1 Place eggs in a medium saucepan with *cold water* to cover by several inches. Bring to a boil. Remove from heat, cover the pot, and let the eggs stand for 12 minutes. Transfer to a bowl of ice water.

2 Peel eggs. Halve them crosswise and carefully scoop yolks out into a bowl. Slice a tiny bit of egg white from rounded sides of egg white halves so they can stand upright. Place egg whites on a platter and reserve.

3 Add half-and-half, mayonnaise, mustard, curry powder, and salt to yolks, and mash to combine. Fold in smoked trout. Add lemon juice and scallions.

4 Spoon mixture into egg whites.

Each serving About 143 calories, 11 g protein, 2 g carbohydrate, 10 g total fat (3 g saturated), 0 g fiber, 212 mg cholesterol, 250 mg sodium.

Use any leftovers to make egg salad: "Scoop the yolk mixture into a bowl. Chop the egg whites and add them to the yolk mixture along with a bit of chopped olives and chopped almonds. Serve on a bed of greens," recommend the Beekman Boys.

Steven Satterfield's Grits Fritters with Country Ham & Cheese

Total time 2 hours plus cooling

Makes about 40 fritters

1 ½ c. whole milk

¾ tsp. kosher salt,
   plus more to taste

1 ½ c. coarse or stone-ground
   grits, rinsed

½ c. heavy cream

6   oz. country ham, finely diced

6   oz. Thomasville Tomme or
    Gouda, rind removed and cut
    into ¼-in. cubes

6   c. canola or peanut oil,
    for frying

⅓ c. all-purpose flour,
    for frying

1   In a medium saucepan over high heat, bring *2 cups water*, milk, and ¾ teaspoon salt to a boil. Reduce heat to medium and slowly add grits in a stream, whisking constantly to avoid lumps.

2   Reduce heat to low and add heavy cream. Cook over low heat, stirring frequently, until grits are completely soft, 50 to 60 minutes. Remove from heat, stir ham into grits, and let grits cool completely. (Grits can be cooked up to a day ahead and stored, covered, in refrigerator.)

3   Using a small ice-cream scoop or a spoon, scoop up about 2 teaspoons grits. Insert a cube of cheese into grits and, using your hands, shape grits around cheese to form a ball. Repeat with remaining grits and cheese.

4   In a large pot fitted with a deep-fry thermometer, heat oil to 350°F over medium-high heat. Preheat oven to 250°F. Place flour on a small plate. In batches of 6, roll fritters in flour to lightly coat, then deep-fry until golden brown, 2 to 3 minutes. Transfer fritters to paper towels to drain. Season with salt, then transfer to a sheet pan in the oven to keep warm until all batches have been fried.

Each serving (4 fritters) About 391 calories, 20 g protein, 26 g carbohydrate, 24 g total fat (7 g saturated), 1 g fiber, 71 mg cholesterol, 845 mg sodium.

Hubert Keller's
Mango-Avocado Bruschetta

Total time 20 minutes

Makes 8 servings (16 bruschetta)

4 Tbsp. extra-virgin
  olive oil, plus more
  for pan and avocado
1 avocado, thinly sliced
1 mango, diced

3 Tbsp. diced red onion
2 Tbsp. fresh lime juice
2 Tbsp. diced red bell pepper
1 Tbsp. chopped fresh cilantro
1 garlic clove, finely chopped

Sea salt and freshly ground
  pepper
1 small baguette, cut into
  16 slices

1   Heat a grill pan over medium-high heat and brush pan and avocado slices with oil. Grill avocado until just charred, about 1 minute per side. Cut into ¼-inch pieces.

2   Preheat oven to 400°F. In a medium bowl, mix avocado, mango, onion, lime juice, bell pepper, cilantro, garlic, and 2 tablespoons oil. Season with salt and pepper.

3   Brush both sides of bread slices with remaining oil. Toast on a baking sheet until golden, about 4 minutes, flipping bread halfway through. Serve toasts topped with mango-avocado mixture.

Each bruschetta About 197 calories, 3 g protein, 22 g carbohydrate, 12 g total fat (1 g saturated), 3 g fiber, 0 mg cholesterol, 168 mg sodium.

Katie Lee's
Italian Stuffed Mushrooms

Total time 40 minutes

Makes 24 mushrooms

½ lb. bulk Italian sweet sausage (or links with casings removed)	⅓ c. grated Parmesan ¼ c. bread crumbs 1 Tbsp. minced parsley	1 lb. white button mushrooms, stems removed

1 Preheat oven to 350°F.

2 In a medium bowl, combine sausage, Parmesan, bread crumbs, and parsley.

3 Lay mushrooms cavity-side up on a large baking sheet and spoon an equal amount of mixture into each cavity.

4 Bake mushrooms for 30 minutes.

Each mushroom About 46 calories, 2 g protein, 2 g carbohydrate, 3 g total fat (1 g saturated), 0 g fiber, 8 mg cholesterol, 95 mg sodium.

"Entertaining at home doesn't have to be a big, scary enterprise. I like to make a selection of easy hors d'oeuvres, and rather than set up a full bar, I serve a signature cocktail . . . and a few bottles of wine. Cheers!"

—Katie Lee

Gregory Gourdet's
Escarole-Chicken Dumplings

Total time 50 minutes

Makes 24 dumplings

¼ c. vegetable oil	3 Tbsp. palm sugar	24 wonton wrappers
9 oz. ground chicken	¼ c. fish sauce	Soy sauce, for dipping
1 (3-in.) piece fresh ginger, minced	4 c. roughly chopped escarole	

1 In a medium pot, heat oil over high heat. Add chicken, ginger, sugar, and fish sauce; cook until liquids are reduced, 5 to 7 minutes. Add escarole and cook until bright green, about 1 minute. Transfer to a paper-towel-lined baking pan to cool, about 20 minutes.

2 Place 1 tablespoon filling in center of 1 wonton wrapper. Moisten edges of wrapper. Pull up 2 opposite corners, then remaining corners, leaving the top open. Repeat with remaining wonton wrappers. Steam dumplings in a steamer until translucent, about 5 minutes. Serve with soy sauce.

Each dumpling About 66 calories, 3 g protein, 6 g carbohydrate, 3 g total fat (0 g saturated), 0 g fiber, 10 mg cholesterol, 290 mg sodium.

Marcus Samuelsson's Farro & Orange Salad (recipe on page 4

Salads & Soups

There's no better addition to a meal than a fresh salad or hearty soup—or that can be the meal all in itself! Whether it's Deborah Madison's Creamy Pea Soup or Rick Bayless' Spinach Salad with Bacon & Roasted Mushrooms, these recipes will satisfy everyone at your table.

Carla Hall's Winter Salad with Pears, Aged Cheddar & Almonds

Total time 20 minutes

Makes 12 servings

Dressing
- ½ c. finely chopped shallots (about 2 large shallots)
- ¼ c. red wine vinegar
- 1 tsp. kosher salt
- ¼ c. extra-virgin olive oil
- ¾ tsp. freshly ground black pepper

Salad
- 2 bunches watercress, thick stems trimmed, cut into 3-in. sprigs (about 8 c.)
- 8 medium heads Belgian endive, halved lengthwise, cut into 1-in. pieces on the bias (about 8 c.)
- 2 large red Bartlett pears, quartered, cored, thinly sliced, tossed in lemon juice
- 2 Tbsp. chopped fresh chives (in ¼-in. pieces)
- 2 Tbsp. coarsely chopped fresh flat-leaf parsley
- ⅔ c. slivered almonds, toasted, coarsely chopped
- ½ c. aged Cheddar, crumbled (about 2 oz.)

1 Prepare dressing: In a glass measuring cup, mix together shallots, vinegar, and salt. Let stand 5 minutes for flavors to meld. Whisk in oil and pepper.

2 Prepare salad: In a bowl, combine watercress, endive, pears, chives, and parsley. Arrange on a platter; sprinkle almonds and cheese on top. Serve dressing on the side.

Each serving About 137 calories, 4 g protein, 11 g carbohydrate, 9 g total fat (2 g saturated), 4 g fiber, 5 mg cholesterol, 202 mg sodium.

Serve the dressing on the side to ensure the greens stay crisp on the buffet. "This salad is so simple," says Carla Hall. "It's toss and go."

John Besh's Louisiana Shrimp Rémoulade with Fall Lettuces

Total time 25 minutes

Makes 8 servings

Shrimp boil
16 c. water
¼ c. sugar
2 Tbsp. Creole spice
1 Tbsp. kosher salt
¼ c. fresh lemon juice
4 bay leaves
1 Tbsp. coriander seeds
1 Tbsp. black peppercorns
2 large fresh thyme sprigs
1 onion, halved

1 head garlic, halved crosswise
32 large shrimp (about 2 lb.), peeled, deveined

Rémoulade
¾ c. mayonnaise
¼ c. Dijon mustard
1 shallot, minced
2 Tbsp. Creole spice
2 Tbsp. white wine vinegar

1½ Tbsp. prepared horseradish, drained
1 tsp. fresh lemon juice
½ tsp. minced garlic
½ tsp. paprika
½ tsp. hot red pepper sauce
¼ tsp. celery salt
8 c. mixed baby greens (such as Lolla Rossa lettuce, green and red oak leaf lettuce, tatsoi, or mizuna)

1   Prepare shrimp boil: In a large pot, bring all ingredients except shrimp to a boil; add shrimp and cook 4 minutes or until just cooked through. Drain; lay out shrimp on a baking sheet and refrigerate to cool.

2   Prepare rémoulade: In a food processor, pulse all ingredients except greens until just blended. Transfer mixture to a large bowl; add shrimp and toss. Refrigerate at least 1 hour or up to 8.

3   To serve, mound salad greens on each plate and top with shrimp.

Each serving About 253 calories, 16 g protein, 6 g carbohydrate, 18 g total fat (2 g saturated), 1 g fiber, 150 mg cholesterol, 1,492 mg sodium.

John Besh appreciates a good wine with dinner. He recommends Stoney Hill Gewürztraminer because "It is very fragrant and goes well with inherent Louisiana."

Rick Bayless' Spinach Salad with Bacon & Roasted Mushrooms

Total time 30 minutes

Makes 8 servings

8 thick slices bacon, cut crosswise into ¼-in.-wide pieces	1 large red onion, sliced into ¼-in.-thick slices	½ tsp. dried oregano, preferably Mexican
4 c. sliced mushrooms (about 8 oz.), preferably shiitakes, oysters, or chanterelles	3 Tbsp. olive oil Juice of 1 lime (about 2 Tbsp.)	½ tsp. salt 8 c. Malabar spinach (about 8 oz.)

1 Preheat oven to 425°F and position a rack in middle of oven. Divide bacon between two baking pans. Scatter mushrooms and onion over bacon. Roast until bacon is crisp, 15 to 20 minutes, stirring halfway through to break up any clumps.

2 Meanwhile, in a small microwave-safe bowl, combine oil, lime juice, oregano, salt, and *2 tablespoons water*. Microwave on High 30 seconds.

3 Place spinach in a large salad bowl. Sprinkle bacon mixture over spinach. Drizzle warm dressing over salad and toss to combine.

Each serving About 208 calories, 5 g protein, 8 g carbohydrate, 18 g total fat (2 g saturated), 2 g fiber, 19 mg cholesterol, 430 mg sodium.

Rick Bayless recommends using a green that will stay solid and says, "Malabar spinach holds up to warm ingredients without losing its texture."

Emeril Lagasse's Roasted Beet Salad with Walnut Dressing & Cheese Crisps

Total time 1 hour 5 minutes plus cooling

3 to 4 small red and/or golden beets, tops discarded, washed

2 Tbsp. plus ½ c. grapeseed or olive oil

½ tsp. salt, plus more for seasoning

¼ tsp. freshly ground black pepper, plus more for seasoning

¼ c. sherry vinegar or Banyuls vinegar (see Note)

1 Tbsp. finely chopped shallot

1 Tbsp. honey

¼ tsp. Dijon mustard

½ c. chopped walnuts, toasted

1 tsp. finely chopped fresh tarragon leaves

1 bunch baby dandelion greens, stems discarded, cut into bite-size pieces (6 c. greens)

1 bunch rainbow chard, stems discarded, cut into bite-size pieces

Cheese Crisps (see recipe on next page)

1   Preheat oven to 350°F.

2   On one half of a 12-inch-square sheet of aluminum foil, place beets, 2 tablespoons oil, *3 tablespoons water*, ¼ teaspoon salt, and ⅛ teaspoon pepper. Fold foil over to cover beets; seal all edges tightly to form a packet. Place packet in jelly-roll pan and bake 45 minutes or until beets are tender when pierced with a paring knife. Let packet stand, unopened, 10 minutes.

3   Remove beets from foil packet. When cool enough to handle, with paper towel, gently rub off skin and discard. Slice beets into ⅛-inch-thick rounds. Transfer to a medium bowl; set aside.

4   In a blender, place vinegar, shallot, honey, mustard, ¼ teaspoon salt, and ⅛ teaspoon pepper and blend until well combined. With blender running, add remaining ½ cup oil in slow, steady stream until dressing is emulsified. Transfer to a small bowl; stir in walnuts and tarragon.

(continued on next page)

5 In a bowl, toss dandelion greens and chard with 2 tablespoons dressing (or more to taste), and season with a pinch of salt and pepper. Add 1 tablespoon dressing to reserved beets; toss gently to coat. Season with a pinch of salt and pepper.

6 To serve, divide dressed greens among six serving plates; garnish with sliced beets and cheese crisps. If desired, spoon more dressing over each salad.

Note: Banyuls vinegar, found in specialty markets, is made from Banyuls wine, which is a fortified wine from southern France that is considered to be the French version of port. Banyuls vinegar has a sweet and nutty flavor that is generally thought to be milder than that of red wine vinegar or balsamic vinegar. It tastes something like a cross between balsamic vinegar and sherry vinegar, and either can be used as a good substitute.

Each serving (without crisps) About 115 calories, 3 g protein, 12 g carbohydrate, 7 g total fat (1 g saturated), 4 g fiber, 0 mg cholesterol, 290 mg sodium.

Emeril's Cheese Crisps

Total time 15 minutes plus cooling   **Makes 12 crisps**

¾ c. shredded hard
   sheep's-milk cheese,
   such as Bianco Sardo

1 Preheat oven to 350°F. Line a cookie sheet with parchment paper.

2 Spoon cheese by measuring tablespoons, 1 to 2 inches apart, onto cookie sheet. Bake 7 to 9 minutes or until cheese melts and turns golden brown.

3 Cool on cookie sheet placed on a wire rack.

Each crisp About 25 calories, 2 g protein, 0 g carbohydrate, 2 g total fat (1 g saturated), 0 g fiber, 5 mg cholesterol, 35 mg sodium.

"Cheese crisps can be made from most hard cheeses, such as Parmigiano-Reggiano, Montasio, and Asiago. They make easy snacks that can be spiced up with dried herbs and spices.

—Emeril Lagasse

Marcus Samuelsson's
Farro & Orange Salad

Total time 50 minutes

Makes 2 servings

½ c. farro
1½ Tbsp. coarsely chopped
     blanched almonds
¼ tsp. fennel seeds
½ fennel bulb, cut into 2 slices
     (¾ in. thick) with core intact
     (reserve any fronds from
     fennel bulb for garnish)

½ small red onion, cut into
     2 slices (½ in. thick)
2 small garlic cloves
2½ Tbsp. olive oil
1 navel orange, segments
     sliced out of membranes,
     juice reserved
1 Tbsp. white balsamic vinegar

½ tsp. each coarse salt and
     freshly ground black pepper
½ small head radicchio, cored,
     finely shredded (1 ½ c.)
2 large fresh basil leaves,
     chopped
4 fresh mint leaves, chopped
1 Tbsp. shaved Parmesan

1 Bring *4 cups salted water* to a boil. Add farro, reduce heat, and simmer 25 minutes or until farro is tender. Drain well and set aside.

2 Meanwhile, in a nonstick skillet over low heat, toast almonds and fennel seeds, tossing until fragrant, about 3 minutes. Set aside.

3 Heat a grill pan over medium heat. Brush fennel, onion, and garlic with ½ tablespoon oil. Grill fennel and onion 12 minutes, turning once, until slightly softened. Grill garlic cloves 5 minutes, turning once, until slightly softened.

4 Dice grilled fennel and onion; transfer to a bowl. Mince garlic; add to grilled vegetables along with farro, remaining oil, orange segments, orange juice, vinegar, salt, and pepper. Gently combine. Add radicchio, basil, and mint; toss again.

5 Arrange a few fennel fronds on two plates. Top with farro salad and Parmesan.

Each serving About 425 calories, 11 g protein, 53 g carbohydrate, 21 g total fat (3 g saturated), 8 g fiber, 2 mg cholesterol, 740 mg sodium.

Lidia Bastianich's
Asparagus & Rice Soup

Total time 2 hours   Makes 8 servings

- **4** large garlic cloves, crushed and peeled
- **⅓** c. plus 2 Tbsp. extra-virgin olive oil
- **2** c. ½-in.-cubed potatoes (about 2 russet potatoes)
- **3** c. chopped leeks, ¼ in. of white and all green parts

- **2** bay leaves
- **1** Tbsp. coarse sea salt or kosher salt, plus more to taste
- **1½** lb. fresh asparagus, cut into ⅓-in. chunks, plus more spears for garnish
- **1** c. Arborio rice

- Freshly ground black pepper, to taste
- **½** c. freshly grated Grana Padano or Parmigiano-Reggiano, plus more to taste

1 In a heavy-bottomed 6-quart pot over medium-high heat, sauté garlic with ⅓ cup oil for 1 to 2 minutes. Add potatoes and cook, stirring occasionally, until crusty but not browned, 4 to 5 minutes. Add leeks and cook until softened, 3 to 4 minutes. Add *5 quarts water*, bay leaves, and 1 tablespoon salt. Stir well, scraping potatoes from pot bottom.

2 Cover, bring to a boil, and add cut asparagus. Lower heat to a vigorous simmer and cook, uncovered, about 1½ hours, stirring occasionally, until reduced by a third. Add rice, bring to a boil, and cook 10 minutes. Remove from heat and season with pepper and more salt to taste. Stir in remaining 2 tablespoons oil and ½ cup grated cheese, or more to taste. If desired, steam remaining asparagus and garnish. Serve hot.

Each serving About 298 calories, 9 g protein, 30 g carbohydrate, 17 g total fat (2 g saturated), 4 g fiber, 9 mg cholesterol, 1,049 mg sodium.

There are nearly as many tricks for getting garlic and onion odors off your hands as there are for getting the smell off your breath. Lidia Bastianich's two favorite solutions: Rub your fingers with crushed fresh parsley or wash hands with lemon juice, then rinse under cold water. And she's got science to back them up: "The garlic enzymes stay on your fingers and continue to release flavors until they're neutralized by an acid, like the lemon juice," Bastianich explains. And parsley causes a similar chemical reaction to knock out the smell.

Lidia Bastianich's Mussel Super Soup

Total time 1 hour 20 minutes

Makes 6 servings

½ lb. carrots, sliced

1 ½ medium (¾ lb.) onions, chopped

2 stalks celery, sliced

1 large clove garlic, crushed with press

1 can (28 oz.) whole tomatoes in juice

¼ small (½ lb.) head green cabbage, thinly sliced

¼ lb. green beans, trimmed and each cut into thirds

1 box (32 oz.) chicken broth

½ tsp. salt

¼ tsp. freshly ground black pepper

2 small (½ lb.) zucchini, sliced into half-moons

1 bag (6 oz.) baby spinach leaves

Pinch of saffron

1 ½ lb. scrubbed and debearded mussels

1   Coat a 12-quart stockpot (or two large saucepans) with *nonstick cooking spray*. Over medium-high heat, add carrots, onions, celery, and garlic; cook 8 minutes or until vegetables soften, stirring occasionally.

2   Add tomatoes with their liquid, breaking up tomatoes with side of a spoon. Add cabbage, green beans, broth, *2 cups water*, salt, and pepper; bring to a boil, stirring occasionally.

3   Reduce heat to low; cover and simmer 10 minutes, stirring occasionally. Increase heat to high; stir in zucchini and spinach and bring to a boil. Reduce heat to low; cover and simmer 10 minutes or until all vegetables are tender.

4   Add saffron and mussels to pot. Bring to a boil, then simmer, covered, 3 minutes, until mussels open.

Each serving About 154 calories, 10 g protein, 25 g carbohydrate, 2 g total fat (0 g saturated), 7 g fiber, 17 mg cholesterol, 1,452 mg sodium.

Lidia Bastianich's
Lentil & Rice Super Soup

Total time 1 hour 20 minutes   Makes 6 servings

½ lb. carrots, sliced
1½ medium (¾ lb.) onions, chopped
2 stalks celery, sliced
1 large clove garlic, crushed with press
1 can (28 oz.) whole tomatoes in juice

¼ small (½ lb.) head green cabbage, thinly sliced
¼ lb. green beans, trimmed and each cut into thirds
1 box (32 oz.) chicken broth
½ tsp. salt
¼ tsp. freshly ground black pepper

2 small (½ lb.) zucchini, sliced into half-moons
1 bag (6 oz.) baby spinach leaves
1 c. cooked or drained, canned lentils
1 c. cooked white rice
2 Tbsp. grated Parmesan

1   Coat a 12-quart stockpot (or two large saucepans) with *nonstick cooking spray*. Over medium-high heat, add carrots, onions, celery, and garlic; cook 8 minutes or until vegetables soften, stirring occasionally.

2   Add tomatoes with their liquid, breaking up tomatoes with side of a spoon. Add cabbage, green beans, broth, *2 cups water*, salt, and pepper; bring to a boil, stirring occasionally.

3   Reduce heat to low; cover and simmer 10 minutes, stirring occasionally. Increase heat to high; stir in zucchini and spinach and bring to a boil. Reduce heat to low; cover and simmer 10 minutes or until all vegetables are tender.

4   Add lentils and rice to pot and heat through. Add Parmesan and more freshly ground black pepper to taste.

Each serving About 192 calories, 9 g protein, 38 g carbohydrate, 1 g total fat (0 g saturated), 9 g fiber, 5 mg cholesterol, 1,421 mg sodium.

Deborah Madison's Creamy Pea Soup

Total time 15 minutes

Makes 4 servings

1 tsp. unsalted butter	1 ½ c. shelled fresh peas	Heavy cream, for garnish
½ small yellow onion, sliced	¾ tsp. salt	
3 c. low-fat chicken broth	½ tsp. sugar	

1   In a medium pot, melt butter. Add onion and cook over medium heat for about 1 minute. Add ½ cup broth and cook for 5 minutes. Add peas, salt, sugar, and remaining 2 ½ cups broth and bring to a boil; reduce heat and simmer for 3 minutes.

2   Puree soup in a blender or food processor until smooth. Serve immediately; garnish with a drizzle of cream.

Each serving About 68 calories, 5 g protein, 10 g carbohydrate, 2 g total fat (1 g saturated), 3 g fiber, 3 mg cholesterol, 903 mg sodium.

Barton Seaver's Linguine with White Clam Sauce & Coriander (recipe on page 61)

Pasta & Risotto

Everybody loves pasta, and celebrity chefs do too. Depending on the recipe, pasta can make a quick and easy weeknight dinner, or a hearty homespun meal worthy of an Italian grandmother. Company coming? Trot out John Besh's Risotto with Pumpkin or Barton Seaver's Linguine with White Clam Sauce & Coriander, and you're sure to impress!

Nigella Lawson's
Pappardelle with Escarole

Total time 20 minutes

Makes 8 main-dish servings

Salt
1 Tbsp. olive oil (preferably garlic-infused)
1 tsp. crushed red pepper flakes

2 heads escarole, roughly chopped
1 c. white wine
1 lb. pappardelle

2 oz. crumbled Parmesan cheese
½ c. chopped fresh flat-leaf parsley

1 Bring a large pot of *salted water* to a boil over high heat. Meanwhile, in a large skillet, heat oil and pepper over medium heat. Add escarole and sauté, stirring occasionally, until it wilts, about 4 minutes. Add wine and *1 cup water*, partially cover pot, and let escarole cook for about 6 minutes.

2 Cook pasta in boiling water for 6 minutes. Drain pasta and add to escarole. Toss; top with Parmesan and parsley. Serve hot.

Each serving About 311 calories, 13 g protein, 46 g carbohydrate, 7 g total fat (2 g saturated), 6 g fiber, 54 mg cholesterol, 152 mg sodium.

Nigella's secret time-saver: garlic-infused oil. "Nearly every time I cook, I start by dribbling this aromatic stuff in a skillet or Dutch oven. It packs instant flavor."

Rachael Ray's Sexy Carbonara

Total time 30 minutes

Makes 6 main-dish servings

Salt
1   lb. pasta, such as spaghetti or
    rigatoni
¼   c. extra-virgin olive oil
    (enough to coat bottom
    of pan)

¼   lb. pancetta (Italian bacon),
    chopped
1   tsp. crushed red pepper
    flakes
5 to 6 garlic cloves, chopped
½   c. dry white wine

2   large egg yolks
Freshly grated Romano
Freshly ground black pepper
Handful of finely chopped fresh
    flat-leaf parsley, for garnish

Rachael Ray knew her boyfriend was the man she should marry when she asked him what he wanted for his birthday dinner. She offered up lobster, steak, and fine foods of all nationalities—but all he wanted was her carbonara. "Carbonara is a bacon-and-egg pasta, a true classic from Italian cuisine," says Rachael. "This is the food of the people!" Admittedly, carbonara isn't exactly health food, especially if you eat a lot of it. But, says Rachael, "Eating it out of the pan or one large bowl with two forks is extra-sexy."

1   Bring a large saucepot of *water* to a boil. Add a liberal amount of salt and the pasta. Cook until al dente, about 8 minutes.

2   Meanwhile, heat a large skillet over medium heat. Add oil and pancetta. Brown pancetta 2 minutes. Add red pepper flakes and garlic and cook 2 to 3 minutes more. Add wine and stir up all the pan drippings.

3   In a separate bowl, beat yolks, then add 1 large ladleful (about ½ cup) pasta cooking water. This tempers the eggs and keeps them from scrambling when added to pasta.

4   Drain pasta well and add it directly to skillet with pancetta and oil. Pour egg mixture over pasta. Toss rapidly to coat pasta without cooking egg. Remove pan from heat and add a big handful of Romano, lots of pepper, and a little salt. Continue to toss and turn pasta until it soaks up egg mixture and thickens, 1 to 2 minutes. Garnish with parsley and extra grated Romano.

Each serving About 516 calories, 19 g protein, 59 g carbohydrate, 22 g total fat (7 g saturated), 4 g fiber, 88 mg cholesterol, 684 mg sodium.

"Usually this recipe makes six servings, but late at night, when no one can see us, my husband John and I eat as much as we want!"

—Rachael Ray

What's Your Quickie Pasta Dish?

"Very simple: penne with butter and Parmesan cheese."

—Scott Conant, owner of Scarpetta restaurants

"Angel hair, sautéed with garlic, lemon, chopped ham, and poppy seeds."

—David Burke, owner of David Burke Townhouse and Fishtail in New York City

"Spaghetti cacio e pepe: I cook pasta, drain it, then put it back in the hot, dry pan with grated Pecorino and coarsely ground pepper and toss it with a little of the pasta cooking liquid."

—Nigella Lawson, author of *Nigellissima*

Mark Bittman's Pasta with Sardines, Bread Crumbs & Capers

Total time 20 minutes

Makes 6 main-dish servings

Salt
¼ c. extra virgin olive oil
½ c. bread crumbs, ideally made
   from stale bread
1 onion, chopped

Freshly ground black pepper
1 lb. long pasta, like perciatelli
1 tsp. grated lemon zest
2 Tbsp. drained capers

2 cans sardines packed
   in extra virgin olive oil
   (about ½ lb.)
½ c. chopped fresh parsley, plus
   more for garnish.

1 Bring a large pot of *water* to a boil and salt it. In a medium skillet over medium heat, add 2 tablespoons oil. When hot, add bread crumbs and cook, stirring frequently, until golden and fragrant, less than 5 minutes, and then remove. Add remaining oil and onion to pan, sprinkle with salt and pepper, and cook, stirring occasionally, until softened, 5 minutes.

2 Meanwhile, add pasta to boiling water and cook until just tender; drain, reserving some of cooking liquid. Turn heat under onions to medium-high and add lemon zest, capers, and sardines; cook, stirring occasionally, until just heated through, 2 minutes.

3 Add pasta to sardine mixture and toss well to combine. Add parsley, most of bread crumbs, and some reserved water, if necessary, to moisten. Taste and adjust seasoning, garnishing with more parsley and bread crumbs.

Each serving About 438 calories, 15 g protein, 61 g carbohydrate, 14 g total fat (2 g saturated), 3 g fiber, 40 mg cholesterol, 323 mg sodium.

"I'm gradually concluding that there are no limits to appealing combinations of dry-pasta-and-whatever, many of them originally created in Southern Italy."

—Mark Bittman

Barton Seaver's Linguine with White Clam Sauce & Coriander

Total time 25 minutes

Makes 4 main-dish servings

1 **bay leaf**	
32 **littleneck clams, washed thoroughly (discard any that won't close)**	

Salt	
1 **lb. linguine**	
2 **strips bacon**	
1 **medium onion, diced**	

1 **tsp. ground coriander**	
1 **c. sour cream**	
2 **Tbsp. chopped fresh flat-leaf parsley**	

1 Place *1 gallon water*, bay leaf, and clams in a large pot and bring to a boil. As the clams begin to open, 5 to 7 minutes, remove them with tongs or a small strainer and set them aside in a bowl. Discard any clams that haven't opened. Strain cooking water into another pot, removing any sand that has accumulated at bottom.

2 Set aside 1 cup cooking water, season remainder lightly with salt, and return to a boil. Add linguine and cook until al dente, following package directions.

3 While waiting for pasta water to boil, combine bacon, onion, coriander, and reserved cup cooking water in a large saucepan. Bring to a boil and continue to cook until reduced by half, about 4 minutes. Remove from heat and whisk in sour cream. Return pan to low heat and warm through. Season to taste with salt and stir in parsley.

4 Drain pasta and add to pan with sauce, along with clams in their shells. Toss to combine and cook over medium heat until pasta has absorbed some sauce, about 2 minutes.

Each serving About 684 calories, 38 g protein, 93 g carbohydrate, 18 g total fat (8 g saturated), 4 g fiber, 84 mg cholesterol, 371 mg sodium.

"I love the classic combination of clams and pasta. I also love coriander, which provides a freshness not often associated with this dish."

—Barton Seaver

Ree Drummond's Chicken Spaghetti

Total time 1 hour 30 minutes

Makes 8 main-dish servings

1 cut-up chicken
1 lb. thin spaghetti, broken into 2-in. pieces
2 cans (10¾ oz. each) cream of mushroom soup
2 ½ c. shredded Cheddar

1 small onion, finely diced
¼ c. finely diced green bell pepper
1 jar (4 oz.) diced pimientos, drained

1 tsp. seasoned salt (such as Lawry's)
Freshly ground black pepper, to taste
⅛ to ¼ tsp. cayenne (ground red) pepper, to taste

Ree Drummond, who writes The Pioneer Woman blog about life with her family and their Oklahoma ranch, says this fabulous casserole is the only one that Marlboro Man (a.k.a., her husband), their cowboys, and their children will eat. Marlboro Man calls it "Mexican Chicken" because of the cayenne pepper, but this dish doesn't usually last long enough for it to matter what anyone calls it.

1 Preheat oven to 350°F. Add chicken to a stockpot. Cover with *water* and bring to a boil. Reduce heat to medium and simmer until chicken is cooked, about 25 minutes.

2 Using tongs or a slotted spoon, remove chicken from water and set aside on a plate to cool.

3 Remove 2 cups broth from pot and set aside. Bring remaining broth back to a boil and add spaghetti. Cook until al dente. Drain and set aside.

4 Using two forks (or your fingers), remove chicken from bones. Shred or cut chicken into bite-size chunks.

5 Place cooked spaghetti in a large bowl. Add soup and 2 cups Cheddar. Then add onion, green pepper, and pimientos. Add seasoned salt, pepper, and cayenne. (Take it easy on the cayenne if you can't handle the heat. But if you can, it sure adds some interest to the final dish.)

6 Add chicken and remaining 2 cups broth. Stir together well, then taste to check seasonings.

7 Pour mixture into a large baking dish and top with remaining ½ cup Cheddar. Bake until bubbly, 35 to 45 minutes.

Each serving About 623 calories, 45 g protein, 50 g carbohydrate, 26 g total fat (11 g saturated), 3 g fiber, 121 mg cholesterol, 1,014 mg sodium.

John Besh's Risotto with Pumpkin

Total time 45 minutes

Makes 8 main-dish servings

2 Tbsp. olive oil	2 to 3 Tbsp. dry white wine	4 to 5 dried porcini mushrooms,
1 medium onion, diced	(optional)	broken into pieces
1 ¼ lb. Musquée de Provence	6 c. chicken broth, heated	2 Tbsp. unsalted butter
or other pumpkin, peeled	1 fresh rosemary sprig,	¾ cup grated Parmesan
and cut into ½-in. cubes	leaves removed and	(about 2 ⅔ oz.)
(about 2 c.)	roughly chopped	Salt and freshly ground pepper,
2 c. Arborio rice		to taste

1 In a large saucepan, heat oil over medium-high heat. Add onion and sauté until soft, about 5 minutes. Add pumpkin and cook, stirring frequently, until softened, 6 to 8 minutes. Add rice, stirring with a wooden spoon until each kernel is coated with oil. Add wine, if desired, and stir until combined.

2 Add 3 cups chicken broth, rosemary, and mushrooms to rice mixture. Bring to a boil, then reduce to a simmer, stirring frequently. As broth is absorbed, add more, ½ cup at a time, stirring frequently—you may not need to use all the broth. Cook until most liquid has been absorbed and rice is slightly al dente, yet creamy and porridgelike, about 18 minutes. Add butter and ¼ cup Parmesan and stir to combine. Season with salt and pepper and serve with remaining Parmesan.

Each serving About 243 calories, 7 g protein, 35 g carbohydrate, 8 g total fat (4 g saturated), 3 g fiber, 12 mg cholesterol, 374 mg sodium.

Mark Bittman's
Pasta with Funghi Trifolati

Total time 25 minutes

Makes 4 main-dish servings

1 oz. dried mushrooms (like cremini, porcini; whatever you like)
Salt
1 Tbsp. olive oil
3 Tbsp. butter
2 tsp. minced garlic

1 medium yellow onion, chopped
1 lb. fresh mushrooms like shiitake or button, sliced (a variety is nice)
½ c. dry white wine or mushroom-soaking liquid

½ lb. cut pasta, like ziti or penne
½ c. fresh chopped parsley, plus more for garnish
Freshly ground black pepper
Fresh-shaved Parmesan (optional)

1 Soak dried mushrooms in very *hot water* until soft, anywhere from 5 to 15 minutes. When tender, remove mushrooms from soaking liquid with a slotted spoon, reserving liquid; slice or chop if pieces are large.

2 Set a large pot of *water* to boil for pasta and salt it. In a large skillet over medium-high heat, add oil and 2 tablespoons butter. When hot, add garlic and onions; cook, stirring occasionally, until onions begin to soften, 3 to 5 minutes. Add fresh mushrooms and dried mushrooms when they're ready, and cook until they give up their liquid and start to brown, at least 15 minutes. Add wine or mushroom-soaking liquid to pot and cook, scraping up any browned bits from the bottom as liquid starts to bubble. Meanwhile, cook pasta until tender.

3 Reduce skillet heat to low. Add remaining butter and parsley, and stir to combine; sprinkle with salt and pepper. When pasta is done, drain. Add pasta to mushroom mixture, and toss until well combined. If mixture is dry, add some pasta water or mushroom-soaking liquid. If you like, garnish with Parmesan and more parsley.

Each serving About 402 calories, 12 g protein, 60 g carbohydrate, 13 g total fat (6 g saturated), 6 g fiber, 23 mg cholesterol, 238 mg sodium.

Bobby Flay's Grilled Salmon with Cherry Tomato, Charred Corn & Basil Relish (recipe on page 70)

Fish & Seafood

You'll love these inventive takes on fish and seafood that your favorite chefs have cooked up. Whether for a family supper or a special occasion, these recipes are sure to please. Try Bobby Flay's Grilled Salmon or Rocco DiSpirito's Shrimp Fra Diavolo and enjoy the compliments that are sure to follow.

Barton Seaver's
Halibut with Ginger-Raisin Crust

Total time 30 minutes

Makes 4 servings

2 ½ Tbsp. butter	3 Tbsp. panko (Japanese-style bread crumbs)	2 tsp. ground mace
¼ c. raisins, chopped into a paste	1 Tbsp. peeled and grated fresh ginger	Grated zest of 1 orange
		2 halibut fillets (5 oz. each)

1 Preheat oven to 300°F. For the coating, melt 2 tablespoons butter and combine with raisin paste in a small bowl. Add panko, ginger, mace, and orange zest and mix well. You should have a thick, slightly sticky paste.

2 Pat halibut as dry as possible, then press the breading paste into the top of the fish and gently massage so it sticks.

3 Heat a large ovenproof sauté pan over medium-high heat. Melt remaining ½ tablespoon butter in pan, then place halibut, breading side down, in butter. Cook, without moving fish, until coating begins to brown around edges, about 4 minutes. Transfer whole pan to oven and cook 20 minutes for a piece of halibut that is 1 ½ inches thick.

4 Once halibut is done, it will begin to flake apart if slight pressure is applied to side. Using a spatula, gently turn fish out of pan and onto serving plates, with breaded side facing up.

Each serving About 248 calories, 26 g protein, 13 g carbohydrate, 10 g total fat (5 g saturated), 1 g fiber, 87 mg cholesterol, 168 mg sodium.

"I love raisins with fish—they have the perfect balance of sweet and acid, which really accentuates the flavors of the not-so-strong-flavored fish, a.k.a. slightly bland-tasting halibut."

—Barton Seaver

Bobby Flay's Grilled Salmon with Cherry Tomato, Charred Corn & Basil Relish

Total time 27 minutes

Makes 4 servings

Relish

- 4 large ears corn on the cob, husk and silk removed
- 1 Tbsp. canola oil
- 1 pt. cherry or grape tomatoes, halved
- 2 Tbsp. balsamic vinegar
- 1 Tbsp. extra-virgin olive oil
- 3 Tbsp. slivered fresh basil leaves
- ½ tsp. kosher salt
- ¼ tsp. freshly ground black pepper

Salmon

- 4 salmon fillets (8 oz. each)
- 1 Tbsp. olive oil
- ½ tsp. kosher salt
- ¼ tsp. freshly ground black pepper
- Slivered fresh basil leaves, for garnish

1 Prepare relish: Heat grill to high. Brush all sides of corn with canola oil. Grill, turning occasionally, until corn is charred and kernels are crisp-tender, about 8 minutes. Set aside until cool enough to handle, then cut kernels from cobs.

2 In a bowl, toss corn, tomatoes, vinegar, olive oil, slivered basil, salt, and pepper. Let stand 15 minutes at room temperature.

3 Prepare salmon: Brush both sides of salmon with oil; season with salt and pepper. Place on grill, skin side down, and grill until golden brown and slightly charred, 3 to 4 minutes. Turn over fillets; grill 2 to 3 minutes longer or until salmon is slightly firm in center and temperature is 140°F on an instant-read thermometer.

4 Serve salmon with relish and garnish with basil leaves.

Each serving About 505 calories, 51 g protein, 31 g carbohydrate, 21 g total fat (4 g saturated), 4 g fiber, 106 mg cholesterol, 621 mg sodium.

What's Always in Your Kitchen?

Avocado: "It's one of my favorite snacks; I halve it and season it with soy sauce, sesame seeds, and lemon juice."

—Rocco DiSpirito, host of *Now Eat This! with Rocco DiSpirito*

Frozen pizza: "I sprinkle it with fresh Parmesan, olive oil, and chili flakes."

—Wolfgang Puck, owner of Spago restaurants

San Marzano canned tomatoes: "I use a can to put together a quick weeknight pasta sauce."

—Ina Garten, host of *Barefoot Contessa*

Sweet Georgia Vidalia onions: "They're the best on the planet. I always have a basketful."

—Trisha Yearwood, host of *Trisha's Southern Kitchen*

Dark chocolate: "I keep 70% on hand as a snack."

—Curtis Stone, host of *Top Chef Masters* and *Around the World in 80 Plates*

Sweet baker's butter: "The higher the fat content the better, because it gives the finished product a richer taste."

—Buddy Valastro, star of *Cake Boss*

Vanilla: "It's my magical ingredient in pancakes and waffles."

—Ree Drummond, host of *The Pioneer Woman*

Mark Bittman's
Last Minute Sort-of Spanish Shrimp

Total time 15 minutes   Makes 2 servings

¼ c. olive oil
1 tsp. chopped garlic
Pinch saffron
1 dried chipotle, left whole

1 tsp. ground cumin
¾ to 1 lb. shrimp, peeled or not
Salt and freshly ground black
   pepper

Chopped parsley and lemon
   wedges for garnish

1   In a skillet just big enough to hold shrimp in one layer over low heat, add oil. Add garlic and adjust heat so it barely sizzles; when it colors nicely, add saffron, chipotle, and cumin, and stir for 1 minute. All seasonings can be adjusted to taste.

2   Add shrimp and season well with salt and pepper. Raise heat a bit and cook, turning once or twice, until firm, 5 minutes or less depending on their size. Garnish and serve.

Each serving About 406 calories, 31 g protein, 3 g carbohydrate, 30 g total fat (4 g saturated), 0 g fiber, 286 mg cholesterol, 1,286 mg sodium.

Katie Lee's
Macadamia Nut–Crusted Tilapia with Pineapple Salsa

Total time 20 minutes

Makes 2 servings

Fish

- ½ c. all-purpose flour
- 1 egg, lightly beaten
- 1 c. crushed macadamia nuts
- 2 tilapia fillets (3 to 4 oz. each)

Salsa

- 1 c. finely chopped fresh pineapple
- 1 Tbsp. minced red onion
- ½ jalapeño, seeds removed, minced
- ¼ c. minced fresh cilantro
- Salt and freshly ground black pepper

1 Prepare fish: Preheat oven to 400°F. Put flour, egg, and nuts in three separate shallow dishes. Dredge each fillet first in flour, then egg, then nuts. Place on *oiled* baking sheet. Bake 12 to 14 minutes, until golden brown. Fish is done when it is opaque and flakes easily with a fork.

2 Prepare salsa: In a medium bowl, combine pineapple, onion, jalapeño, and cilantro. Season with salt and pepper. Serve with fish.

Each serving About 793 calories, 36 g protein, 45 g carbohydrate, 56 g total fat (10 g saturated), 8 g fiber, 146 mg cholesterol, 238 mg sodium.

Barton Seaver's Pink Salmon Cakes with Dill & Mustard

Total time 20 minutes

2 cans pink salmon
  (7–8 oz. each)
Salt
2 Tbsp. mayonnaise

2 tsp. whole-grain mustard
Pinch ground mace
¼ c. panko (Japanese-style
  bread crumbs)

2 Tbsp. chopped fresh dill
3 Tbsp. butter
Lemon wedges

1 Preheat oven to 400°F. Drain salmon. Flake fish into a bowl, being careful to remove any small bones or skin that may be mixed in.

2 Season with salt and add mayonnaise, mustard, mace, bread crumbs, and dill. Mix gently with your fingers until it is well combined.

3 Form fish mixture into 4 even patties, about 1 inch thick, and let sit for about 5 minutes to allow bread crumbs to absorb flavor.

4 In a large, oven-safe sauté pan over medium heat, heat butter until foaming. Add salmon cakes and cook until they begin to turn golden on the edges, about 5 minutes. Don't touch them while they're browning.

5 Once edges have browned, transfer pan to oven and bake for 5 minutes to heat through. Flip cakes onto plates and serve with lemon wedges.

Each serving About 300 calories, 20 g protein, 5 g carbohydrate, 23 g total fat (8 g saturated), 0 g fiber, 88 mg cholesterol, 667 mg sodium.

"This has become a weeknight favorite at our house. The cakes are inexpensive and easy to put together. Add a side dish, and you have dinner for four."

—Barton Seaver

Rocco DiSpirito's Shrimp Fra Diavolo (Farfalle with Shrimp)

Total time 40 minutes

Makes 4 servings

2 tsp. salt, plus more for seasoning

2 oz. whole-wheat farfalle, such as Delallo

1 Tbsp. extra-virgin olive oil

8 garlic cloves, thinly sliced

⅛ tsp. crushed red pepper flakes

¼ c. roughly chopped fresh flat-leaf parsley

1 Tbsp. red wine vinegar

2 c. canned plum tomatoes, drained but not squeezed

1¼ lb. extra-large fresh shrimp, peeled and deveined

Freshly ground black pepper, for seasoning

1 In a large pot, bring *4 quarts water* to a boil and add 2 teaspoons salt. Add farfalle and cook according to package directions, about 8 minutes for al dente. Drain farfalle and set aside.

2 In a large nonstick skillet, heat oil over medium-high heat. Add garlic and cook, stirring, until it turns golden brown, about 2 minutes. Add red pepper flakes and parsley and cook 10 seconds. Add vinegar and cook until most of it evaporates. Squeeze tomatoes into pan with your hands and cook until almost all liquid is evaporated.

3 Season shrimp with salt and pepper; add to skillet, cover, and turn off heat to let shrimp gently heat through, 6 to 8 minutes. Add farfalle, turn heat to medium, and bring to a simmer.

4 Using a slotted spoon, divide shrimp among four bowls. Spoon sauce around shrimp.

Each serving About 218 calories, 23 g protein, 19 g carbohydrate, 5 g total fat (1 g saturated), 3 g fiber, 179 mg cholesterol, 1,140 mg sodium.

Fresh herbs can add a lot of bang for your buck. Rocco DiSpirito says, "There's no dish—other than chocolate mousse—that won't be improved by fresh herbs."

Sara Foster's Chicken Potpie (recipe on page 82)

Poultry

Poultry is often the centerpiece of an elaborate meal, but it can also be the fastest and healthiest way to get dinner on the table during the week. Bobby Flay's spicy fried chicken is great for feeding a crowd and Lisa Fain's enchiladas will add Mexican flair to any weeknight dinner. And for that elaborate meal? Try Emeril Lagasse's Pan-Roasted Duck Breasts with Apple Cider Reduction.

Lisa Fain's
Sour Cream–Chicken Enchiladas

Total time 1 hour 30 minutes   **Makes 8 servings**

3	lb. boneless, skinless chicken breasts	
Kosher salt and freshly ground black pepper		
4	Tbsp. olive oil	
2	Tbsp. unsalted butter, plus more for baking dish	

2	serrano chiles, seeds and stems removed, diced
2	garlic cloves, minced
2	Tbsp. all-purpose flour
2	c. chicken broth
2	c. sour cream
1	c. chopped fresh cilantro
1	tsp. ground cumin

Dash of cayenne (ground red) pepper	
1	can (11 oz.) tomatillos, drained
24	corn tortillas
10	oz. Monterey Jack, grated (2½ c.)
1	medium onion, diced

This casserole is a perfect make-ahead dish. "These enchiladas are great for parties: Make them up to a day in advance, then pop the pan in the oven as guests are settling in," says Lisa Fain.

1   Preheat oven to 350°F. Season chicken with salt and pepper, toss with 2 tablespoons oil, and bake in a cast-iron skillet until cooked through, about 30 minutes. Let cool, shred, and set aside.

2   Meanwhile, in a large pot over medium-low heat, melt butter. Add chiles; cook until soft, about 4 minutes. Add garlic; cook for 1 minute. Whisk in flour for 1 minute. Whisk in broth until thickened, about 6 minutes. Stir in sour cream, ¼ cup cilantro, cumin, and cayenne. Transfer to a blender, add tomatillos, and puree. Pour 1 cup mixture in each of two buttered 9" by 13" baking dishes.

3   In a large skillet over medium heat, heat 1½ teaspoons oil and cook tortillas in batches until soft, about 1 minute per side, adding remaining oil as needed. Place ¼ cup reserved chicken, 1 tablespoon cheese, and 1 teaspoon onion on each tortilla and roll into a cigar shape. Place in baking dishes and cover with remaining sour-cream mixture and cheese. Bake until top is lightly browned, about 25 minutes. Garnish with remaining cilantro.

Each serving About 694 calories, 51 g protein, 39 g carbohydrate, 37 g total fat (16 g saturated), 6 g fiber, 173 mg cholesterol, 768 mg sodium.

Sara Foster's Chicken Potpie

Total time 2 hours 20 minutes

Makes 10 servings

1 **chicken (4 to 4½ lb.)**	
12 **Sara Foster's Herb Biscuits, uncooked (recipe at right)**	
6 **Tbsp. unsalted butter**	
4 **carrots, peeled and chopped**	

4 **celery stalks, chopped**
8 **oz. fresh button mushrooms, thinly sliced**
¼ **c. all-purpose flour**
1 **box (10 oz.) frozen green peas**

1 **Tbsp. chopped fresh sage**
Salt and freshly ground pepper to taste
1 **egg**
2 **Tbsp. milk**

"'Comforting' is the best way to describe my mom's cooking," says Sara Foster. Raised in Jackson, Tennessee, this Southern chef grew up eating slow-cooked vegetables and big family meals prepared by her mother, Say. Of all her mom's dishes, Foster's favorite remains chicken potpie, filled with mushrooms, carrots, and peas and topped with flaky biscuits. "My mom never used recipes," says Foster. "After I moved away, she'd talk me through the steps on the phone, saying things like, 'Add flour until it looks like the right consistency.' She still cooks by memory today."

1 Place chicken in a large pot and add enough *water* to cover by 1 inch. Bring to a boil over medium-high heat. Reduce heat to low and simmer until meat is fully cooked, about 45 minutes. Meanwhile, prepare biscuits according to recipe directions and set aside.

2 Remove chicken from pot and reserve 5 cups cooking liquid. When chicken is cool enough to handle, pull off meat in large chunks. Set aside.

3 Preheat oven to 375°F. In a large skillet, melt butter over medium-high heat and add carrots, celery, and mushrooms. Sauté, stirring frequently, about 10 minutes. Add flour and cook, stirring, until flour is light brown, 3 to 4 minutes. Slowly whisk in reserved cooking liquid and bring to a low boil while whisking. Add peas and sage. Season with salt and pepper, reduce heat, and simmer, stirring occasionally, until thick, 10 to 15 minutes. Add chicken meat, remove from heat, and transfer mixture into a 9" by 13" baking dish.

4 Top with biscuits. In a small bowl, beat egg and milk together and lightly brush over biscuits. Bake potpie until biscuits are golden brown and chicken mixture is bubbling around edges, 25 to 30 minutes. Serve immediately.

Each serving About 839 calories, 40 g protein, 45 g carbohydrate, 55 g total fat (19 g saturated), 4 g fiber, 200 mg cholesterol, 762 mg sodium.

Sara Foster's Herb Biscuits

Total time 15 minutes   **Makes 1 dozen 2 ½–in. biscuits**

3 ½ c. all-purpose flour,
  plus more for dusting
2 tsp. baking powder
1 tsp. baking soda
1 tsp. salt

1 c. (2 sticks) cold unsalted
  butter, cut into small cubes
2 Tbsp. chopped fresh
  flat-leaf parsley
1 ½ c. buttermilk

1 Lightly flour a baking sheet and set aside. Sift flour, baking powder, baking soda, and salt together into a large bowl. Cut butter into flour mixture, using a pastry blender or two knives, until mixture is coarse and crumbly. Stir in parsley.

2 Make a well in center of flour mixture, pour in buttermilk, and use a fork to stir until dough just comes together—do not overmix. Turn onto a lightly floured surface and pat or roll dough into a circle about ½ inch thick. Cut out biscuits using a floured 2 ½-inch-round cutter.

3 Transfer biscuits to baking sheet, cover with waxed paper, and set aside until ready to use.

Bobby Flay's 16-Spice Fried Chicken with Mango–Red Chile Honey

Total time 1 hour 40 minutes plus marinating

Makes 8 main-dish servings

1 Tbsp. ancho chile powder	2 tsp. onion powder	4 tsp. kosher salt
1 Tbsp. ground coriander	1 tsp. ground allspice	2 ½ tsp. freshly ground
1 Tbsp. ground cumin	1 tsp. ground cinnamon	black pepper
1 Tbsp. ground ginger	1 tsp. ground cloves	2 chickens (about 3 lb. each),
1 Tbsp. pasilla chile powder	1 tsp. ground fennel seeds	each cut into 8 pieces
(or 2 tsp. ancho chile powder	½ tsp. cayenne (ground red)	6 c. low-fat buttermilk
plus 1 tsp. crushed red	pepper	1 ½ c. mango nectar
pepper)	½ tsp. plus ⅛ tsp. ground	½ c. clover honey
1 Tbsp. brown sugar	chile de árbol or crushed red	6 c. canola oil
2 tsp. garlic powder	pepper	3 c. all-purpose flour

1 In a bowl, combine ancho chile powder, coriander, cumin, ginger, pasilla chile powder, sugar, garlic powder, onion powder, allspice, cinnamon, cloves, fennel, cayenne, ½ teaspoon chile de árbol, 2 teaspoons salt, and 2 teaspoons black pepper.

2 Place chicken on a jelly-roll pan. Season with spice mixture. Cover and refrigerate for at least 1 hour or up to 8 hours.

3 Transfer chicken to a 3-quart baking dish. Pour 4 cups buttermilk over chicken, turning to coat. Cover; refrigerate at least 4 hours or up to 24 hours.

4 In a 2-quart saucepan, boil mango nectar over high heat until reduced to ¼ cup. Stir in honey, ⅛ teaspoon chile de árbol, and ¼ teaspoon salt. Let cool.

5 Remove chicken from refrigerator; let stand 30 minutes. Pour oil into a 2-inch-deep 12-inch cast-iron skillet (or a Dutch oven) to reach 1 inch up side. Heat over medium heat until oil reaches 350°F on deep-fry thermometer. Preheat oven to 375°F.

6 Transfer chicken from buttermilk marinade to large cutting board; pat dry with paper towels. Discard marinade.

7 Into a 2-quart baking dish, pour remaining 2 cups buttermilk; whisk in ¼ teaspoon salt and ¼ teaspoon black pepper. In another 2-quart baking dish, place flour. Stir in ½ teaspoon salt and ¼ teaspoon black pepper.

8 Working with breasts and thighs, dip chicken into buttermilk mixture, allowing excess to drip off; then dip into flour mixture to coat, tapping off excess. In batches, carefully place chicken in hot oil, making sure not to crowd the skillet.

9 Fry breasts and thighs, turning occasionally, 10 to 12 minutes or until golden brown and cooked through (165°F). If some pieces turn golden brown before insides have reached 165°F, transfer to a rack fitted inside an 18" by 12" jelly-roll pan and bake for 4 to 8 minutes or until cooked through (165°F). Sprinkle chicken with ½ teaspoon salt. Reduce oven temperature to 200°F. Keep chicken warm in pan in oven.

10 Repeat breading process with wings and drumsticks. In batches, fry, turning occasionally, 6 to 9 minutes or until golden brown and cooked through. Transfer cooked pieces to prepared pan in oven. Season with ½ teaspoon salt. Serve with mango-honey sauce.

Each serving About 660 calories, 49 g protein, 47 g carbohydrate, 30 g total fat (7 g saturated), 2 g fiber, 144 mg cholesterol, 790 mg sodium.

Ming Tsai's
Cranberry-Hoisin Chicken Rice

Total time 1 hour   **Makes 4 servings**

2 **Tbsp. canola oil**	2 **Tbsp. minced garlic**	3 **c. low-sodium**
8 **bone-in chicken thighs,**	2 **c. jasmine rice**	**chicken stock**
skin on	¼ **c. hoisin sauce**	1 **c. fresh cranberries**
2 **bunches scallions, sliced**	1 **c. dry red wine**	

1   Preheat oven to 375°F. In a Dutch oven, heat oil over medium-high heat. Brown chicken on both sides. Set aside.

2   In same pot, sauté scallions and garlic. Add rice and sauté 1 minute. Add hoisin and stir, then add red wine and cook, stirring occasionally, until liquid is reduced by three-quarters, about 2 minutes.

3   Add stock, cranberries, and chicken to pot and bring to a simmer; cover and bake for 30 minutes. Let rest 10 minutes before serving.

Each serving About 1,004 calories, 47 g protein, 121 g carbohydrate, 31 g total fat (9 g saturated), 6 g fiber, 116 mg cholesterol, 1,200 mg sodium.

Emeril Lagasse's
Pan-Roasted Duck Breasts
with Apple Cider Reduction

Total time 1 hour 25 minutes   **Makes 2 servings**

2 c. apple cider or pressed
  apple juice
2 c. beef stock or
  low-sodium beef broth
1 cinnamon stick (3 in. long)

4 whole cloves
4 black peppercorns
⅔ c. sliced shallot
2 duck-breast halves
  with skin (8 oz. each)

½ tsp. kosher salt
½ tsp. freshly ground
  black pepper
1 tsp. olive oil

1   In a 2-quart saucepan, combine cider or juice, beef stock or broth, cinnamon stick, cloves, peppercorns, and shallot and bring to a boil over medium-high heat. Cook 50 to 55 minutes or until reduced to 1 cup, including seasoning. Let cool slightly, then strain through a fine-mesh sieve set over a small bowl, discarding shallot and spices. Set aside.

2   Pat duck-breast halves dry with paper towels. With a knife, cut 4 diagonal slices through skin and fat of each half. Sprinkle breasts with ½ teaspoon each salt and pepper. In a 12-inch skillet, heat oil over medium heat. Add duck, skin side down; cook 2 minutes. Reduce heat to medium-low; cook 10 to 12 minutes longer or until skin is golden brown and crisp and most of fat has been rendered. Carefully drain off most of fat. Turn duck over. Increase heat to medium; cook 5 to 6 minutes for medium-rare, or to desired doneness.

Each serving About 331 calories, 31 g protein, 22 g carbohydrate, 12 g total fat (3 g saturated), 0 g fiber, 154 mg cholesterol, 750 mg sodium.

"This recipe was developed for domesticated duck. But if you enjoy the deep flavor of wild duck (and have access to it), you could adapt it by searing the breasts very quickly in the pan over high heat (taking care not to overcook them, since wild ducks are typically very lean)."

—Emeril Lagasse

John Besh's Pecan-Baked Ham (recipe on page 9[...])

Meat

A well-cooked piece of meat, whether it's beef, pork, or lamb, is an easy way to impress your family and guests. John Besh's Pecan-Baked Ham is sure to make any holiday meal an instant classic, and Ree Drummond's Comfort Meatballs will definitely become a household favorite. Want to wow your spouse or partner? Cook up Marcus Samuelsson's Miso-Rubbed Rack of Lamb plus Collard Greens and you'll never hear the end of it.

Rocco DiSpirito's Steak Pizzaiola

Total time 45 minutes

Makes 4 servings

---

4   pieces hanger steak
    (6 oz. each), trimmed
    of excess fat and sinew
Salt
Freshly ground black pepper
1   Tbsp. extra-virgin olive oil

8   garlic cloves, thinly sliced
1   small onion, sliced
    ½ in. thick
1   Tbsp. chopped fresh oregano
2   red bell peppers, sliced
    ½ in. thick

1   cubanelle pepper,
    sliced ½ in. thick
1   c. chopped tomatoes
    with no fat, sodium, or sugar
    added, such as Pomi
⅛   tsp. crushed red pepper
    flakes (optional)

1   Preheat oven to 350°F. Place a wire rack over a baking sheet.

2   Pat steaks dry with paper towels; season with salt and pepper. Pour oil into a large ovenproof skillet, place over high heat, and heat until smoking. Add steaks and brown each side evenly, about 2 minutes per side. Remove steaks from pan and let rest on wire rack.

3   Reduce heat to medium. Add garlic to pan and cook, stirring, until browned, about 2 minutes. Add onion, oregano, and peppers and cook until softened, about 3 minutes. Add chopped tomatoes and cook until tomatoes form a sauce around peppers, 4 to 5 minutes.

4   Place steaks on top of tomato-and-pepper mixture, cover, and place in oven. Cook for about 5 minutes for medium-rare to medium doneness. Remove meat from sauce and let rest on the rack again.

5   Cook tomato sauce down until it is thick, about 8 minutes, then stir in red pepper flakes, if desired.

6   Cut each steak into three chunks and divide among four plates. Spoon sauce over and around meat.

Each serving About 369 calories, 38 g protein, 13 g carbohydrate, 18 g total fat (6 g saturated), 4 g fiber, 111 mg cholesterol, 268 mg sodium.

To ensure tender results, age your beef for five days in red wine. The natural enzymes will tenderize the meat.

Sandra Lee's
Hungarian Veal

Total time 8 to 10 hours

Makes 6 servings

2½ pounds veal stew meat
or veal roast, cut into
bite-size pieces
1 package (8-ounce) presliced
fresh mushrooms
1 cup frozen chopped onion

1 cup frozen loose-pack
crinkle-cut sliced carrots
1 cup reduced-sodium
chicken broth
2 packages (0.75 ounces each)
mushroom gravy mix

2 tablespoons Hungarian
sweet paprika
1 teaspoon bottled
crushed garlic
Hot cooked egg noodles
(optional)
Fresh herbs sprigs (optional)

1   In a 4- to 5-quart slow cooker, stir together veal, mushrooms, onion, carrots, chicken broth, gravy mix, paprika, and garlic.

2   Cover and cook on LOW heat setting for 8 to 10 hours.

3   Serve over cooked egg noodles and top with herb sprigs (optional).

Each serving About 263 calories, 41 g protein, 9 g carbohydrate, 6 g total fat (2 g saturated), 2 g fiber, 159 mg cholesterol, 607 mg sodium.

The secret
to authentic
Hungarian
goulash is slow
cooking and
plenty of paprika.
Use Hungarian
paprika—it's
sweeter—and buy
the mushrooms
presliced.

John Besh's Pecan-Baked Ham

Total time 2 hours 15 minutes

1 c. packed brown sugar	1 Tbsp. Chinese five-spice powder	2 medium onions, chopped
¼ c. finely chopped pecans	1 good-quality cooked ham (5 lb.)	
2 Tbsp. unsalted butter, softened		

1 Preheat oven to 350°F. In a small bowl, mix brown sugar, pecans, butter, and five-spice powder to create a fine, crumbly mixture. Using your hands, rub mixture onto ham.

2 In the bottom of a heavy roasting pan, scatter onions; then add *2 cups water*. Place ham atop bed of onions and roast until glaze is glistening and deep brown, 1 hour 40 minutes to 2 hours, checking occasionally to make sure water hasn't evaporated (add ¼ to ½ cup more, as needed).

3 Slice ham and top with pan juices, including onions. If sauce is too thin, pour liquid into a medium saucepan and reduce over medium-high heat until desired consistency is achieved.

Each serving About 448 calories, 43 g protein, 21 g carbohydrate, 21 g total fat (7 g saturated), 1 g fiber, 117 mg cholesterol, 2,841 mg sodium.

"The tradition of the Sunday feast accomplishes more than just feeding us, it nurtures us."

—John Besh

Marcus Samuelsson's Miso-Rubbed Rack of Lamb plus Collard Greens

Total time 50 minutes

Makes 2 servings

1	Tbsp. miso paste		1	rack of lamb (1½ lb.),		1	Tbsp. olive oil	

- 1 Tbsp. miso paste
- 1½ tsp. butter, softened
- 1½ tsp. chopped fresh sage
- 1½ tsp. mild chili powder
- 1½ tsp. stirred egg yolk

- 1 rack of lamb (1½ lb.), with bones frenched
- ½ tsp. coarse salt
- ½ tsp. coarsely ground black pepper

- 1 Tbsp. olive oil
- ¼ c. panko (Japanese-style bread crumbs)
- Collard Greens (see recipe on next page)

1 Heat oven to 400°F.

2 In a small bowl, stir miso, butter, sage, chili powder, and egg yolk until blended. Set aside.

3 Season lamb all over with salt and pepper. In a large ovenproof skillet, heat oil over medium-high heat. Add lamb and sear until browned, 3 minutes per side. Remove from heat; cool slightly. Smear miso mixture onto lamb. Press panko into miso mixture on rounded side of lamb.

4 Place skillet in oven; roast until an instant-read thermometer inserted into center of rack registers 130°F, 20 to 25 minutes. Place lamb on a cutting board and let rest 5 minutes.

5 Cut rack into 4 double chops. Serve with collard greens.

Each serving without collards About 534 calories, 28 g protein, 13 g carbohydrate, 41 g total fat (16 g saturated), 1 g fiber, 158 mg cholesterol, 970 mg sodium.

Marcus Samuelsson's
Collard Greens

Total time 40 minutes   **Makes 2 servings**

½ **lb. collard greens,** center ribs removed, thinly sliced (2 c.)	1 ½ **tsp. soy sauce**
½ **lb. baby bok choy,** thinly sliced (2 c.)	1 ½ **tsp. whole-grain Dijon mustard**
2 **slices bacon**	1 **large garlic clove,** thinly sliced
⅓ **c. unsweetened coconut milk**	1 ½ **tsp. unsalted butter**

World-famous chef Marcus Samuelsson cooked this dish for his wife, model Maya Haile, as part of a Valentine's Day meal. "Watching him cook is sexy because he's so passionate," Maya says. "He's different when he's cooking—he's totally focused and ready to work. But outside the kitchen, he's just a sweet man." She's willing to return the favor, especially when it comes to cooking classics from their native country: "She's better at cooking Ethiopian food than I am," says Marcus.

1 In a 2-quart saucepan, bring *6 cups salted water* to a boil. Add greens and cook until crisp-tender, 3 to 4 minutes. Lift greens from water with a sieve and drain on a paper towel. Add bok choy to boiling water; blanch 30 seconds. Scoop bok choy from water and drain on a separate paper towel.

2 In a large nonstick skillet, cook bacon until crisp, about 7 minutes; drain on a paper towel. Leave drippings in skillet.

3 In a small bowl, whisk together coconut milk, soy sauce, and mustard.

4 Add garlic to drippings in skillet and cook over medium-low heat until garlic is pale golden brown, about 5 minutes. Remove garlic from skillet with a slotted spoon and drain on paper towel with bacon.

5 Add butter to skillet and melt over medium heat. Add greens and sauté 3 minutes or until crisp-tender. Stir in coconut mixture and simmer over medium-low heat 3 minutes longer or until collards are just tender. Stir in bok choy and cook 1 minute longer, or until heated through. Crumble bacon and stir into greens along with garlic. Spoon greens onto two plates and top with lamb chops.

Each serving About 237 calories, 6 g protein, 8 g carbohydrate, 22 g total fat (12 g saturated), 3 g fiber, 23 mg cholesterol, 701 mg sodium.

Ree Drummond's Comfort Meatballs

Total time 1 hour 30 minutes

Makes 8 servings

Meatballs

1½ lb. ground beef
¾ c. quick oats
1 c. milk
3 Tbsp. very finely minced
  onion

1 ½ tsp. salt
Plenty of freshly ground
  black pepper
4 Tbsp. canola oil
½ c. flour

Sauce

1 c. ketchup
2 Tbsp. sugar
3 Tbsp. distilled white vinegar
2 Tbsp. Worcestershire sauce
4 to 6 Tbsp. minced onion
Dash of Tabasco

1 Prepare meatballs: In a bowl, combine the ground beef and oats. Pour in milk, then add onion and salt. Add pepper to taste, then stir to combine. Roll mixture into tablespoon-size balls and refrigerate 30 to 45 minutes.

2 Heat oven to 350°F. In a large skillet, heat oil over medium heat. Spread flour on a plate. Dredge meatballs in flour, then brown them in batches until light brown. As they brown, place them in a rectangular baking dish.

3 Prepare sauce: In a bowl, stir together all ingredients and drizzle over meatballs.

4 Bake until bubbly and hot, about 45 minutes.

Each serving About 316 calories, 18 g protein, 25 g carbohydrate, 16 g total fat (5 g saturated), 1 g fiber, 56 mg cholesterol, 869 mg sodium.

"If you'd like to serve with pasta, egg noodles tossed in a little melted butter would be divine," suggests Ree Drummond.

Bobby Flay's Pulled Pork with Black Pepper Vinegar

Total time 9 hours 30 minutes plus marinating

Makes 12 servings

⅓ c. ancho chile powder
2 Tbsp. sweet Spanish (smoked) paprika
1 Tbsp. ground oregano
1 Tbsp. ground coriander
1 Tbsp. dry mustard
1 tsp. ground cumin

½ tsp. chile de árbol powder or cayenne (ground red) pepper
4 ½ tsp. kosher salt
2 ½ tsp. freshly ground black pepper
1 bone-in pork shoulder (5 to 6 lb.), trimmed

½ c. rice vinegar
¼ c. Dijon mustard
1 Tbsp. honey
¾ c. plus 2 Tbsp. canola oil
12 hamburger buns, lightly toasted

1 In a small bowl, combine all spices and 1 teaspoon each salt and pepper.

2 Place pork on a jelly-roll pan. Season with 2 teaspoons salt and ½ teaspoon pepper; rub spice mixture all over pork. Cover and refrigerate at least 1 hour or up to 8 hours.

3 Following manufacturer's instructions, start fire for a smoker with lump charcoal and ½ cup drained soaked wood chips. Bring temperature of smoker to 225° to 250°F. Or, follow directions on page 102 to turn your grill into a smoker.

4 In smoker, set pork on rack; cover and cook, turning hourly, until meat thermometer inserted into center of pork registers 165°F, 6 to 9 hours. Add more charcoal as needed to maintain temperature, and more drained wood chips to maintain smoke level.

5 Meanwhile, in a blender, puree vinegar, mustard, honey, 1½ teaspoons salt, and 1 teaspoon pepper. With blender running, add oil in a slow stream until emulsified. Sauce can be refrigerated for up to 3 days.

6 Transfer pork to a clean pan; cool slightly. Shred meat into bite-size pieces, discarding bone and fat. Mound meat on platter; drizzle with some vinegar sauce and any accumulated pan juices. Serve pork on buns with remaining sauce.

Slow cooker variation: Proceed as instructed in steps 1 and 2. Place pork in 6-quart slow cooker bowl. Add 1 can (14 ounces) lower-sodium chicken broth. Cook, covered, on Low 10 to 12 hours or until tender when pierced with tip of knife and cooked through (165°F). Continue with steps 5 and 6.

Each serving About 725 calories, 52 g protein, 29 g carbohydrate, 44 g total fat (11 g saturated), 3 g fiber, 170 mg cholesterol, 1,195 mg sodium.

Transform Your Grill into a Smoker

There's nothing like the taste of smoked meat or fish. Don't have a smoker? Flay says your grill can do the job. His advice:

1 In the bottom of your grill, set up two zones: Place charcoal on one side only. Add presoaked wood chips on top of briquettes; these will create the smoke. "For meats and chicken, I use hickory," Flay says. "For fish and vegetables, I use cherrywood." Light the charcoal; Flay uses a chimney starter, never fluid. "Lighter fluid should not be anywhere near your house," he says—if it is, "the food will taste like it."

2 Place a grill-safe pan of water on top of the charcoal and wood chips to create steam.

3 Put the meat, fish, or other ingredients on the side of the grill without charcoal, where there's no direct heat. "What you're getting is steam heat and smoke that's low and slow," says Flay. Let food smoke (about 10 hours for a pork shoulder), monitoring it regularly.

Sandra Lee's
Five-Spice Beef Stew

Total time 8 to 10 hours

Makes 6 servings

2 pounds beef stew meat, cut into 1-inch pieces	2 cans (14.5 ounces each) diced tomatoes with onion and garlic, S&W®	1 tablespoon five-spice powder, McCormick®
1 pound baby carrots	¾ cup reduced-sodium beef broth, Swanson®	Salt and ground black pepper
		Hot mashed potatoes (optional)

1 In a 4- to 5-quart slow cooker, stir together beef stew meat, carrots, undrained tomatoes, beef broth, and five-spice powder until thoroughly combined.

2 Cover and cook on LOW heat setting for 8 to 10 hours. Season with salt and pepper.

3 Serve with mashed potatoes (optional).

Each serving About 279 calories, 36 g protein, 18 g carbohydrate, 7 g total fat (3 g saturated), 3 g fiber, 97 mg cholesterol, 665 mg sodium.

Wolfgang Puck's
Shepherd's Pies with Lamb

Total time 1 hour 35 minutes

Makes 8 servings

2 **Tbsp. olive oil**	1 **c. frozen peas**	¼ **c. milk, plus more if needed**
1½ **lb. ground lamb**	1½ **c. beef gravy**	2 **Tbsp. freshly grated**
3 **carrots, cut into ¼-in. rounds**	**Kosher salt and freshly ground**	**horseradish**
2 **leeks, cut into ¼-in. rounds**	**black pepper**	2 **slices country white bread,**
½ **lb. red Swiss chard, thick ribs**	1½ **lb. russet potatoes, peeled**	**crusts removed, bread cut**
removed, leaves	**and cut into 2½-in. rounds**	**into 2-in. pieces**
cut into 2-in. pieces	5 **Tbsp. unsalted butter**	2 **oz. Parmesan, grated (½ c.)**

1   In a large skillet, heat 1 tablespoon oil over medium heat. Add lamb and cook until browned, about 8 minutes. Transfer lamb to a bowl and set aside. In same skillet, add remaining oil, carrots, and leeks and cook until softened, about 5 minutes. Stir in Swiss chard and cook 2 minutes. Stir in peas, gravy, and reserved lamb. Season with salt and pepper. Reduce heat to medium-low and cook until heated through, about 10 minutes. Remove from heat and cover.

2   Preheat oven to 350°F. In a large pot add potatoes and enough *salted water* to cover and bring to a boil over high heat. Reduce heat to medium and simmer until potatoes are tender, about 20 minutes. Drain potatoes and return to pot. Add 3 tablespoons butter and mash potatoes. Stir in milk and season with salt. If potatoes are too stiff, add up to 2 tablespoons more milk. Stir in horseradish.

3   Transfer lamb mixture to eight 4-inch ramekins or an 11-inch deep-dish pie plate. Spread mashed potatoes over lamb mixture.

4   In a food processor, pulse bread to crumbs. Sprinkle crumbs and Parmesan on potatoes. Dot with remaining butter. Bake until tops are lightly browned, about 45 minutes.

Each serving About 524 calories, 30 g protein, 32 g carbohydrate, 31 g total fat (15 g saturated), 4 g fiber, 110 mg cholesterol, 566 mg sodium.

"When I cook a romantic meal for my wife, Gelila, I'll finish it with chocolate soufflé. And she needs good wine and champagne."

—Wolfgang Puck

Amanda Freitag's Strip Steak with Herb Butter & Tomatoes

Total time 25 minutes

Makes 4 servings

1   c. fresh flat-leaf parsley, stems removed, leaves coarsely chopped
2   shallots, peeled and chopped
½   c. (1 stick) unsalted butter, softened

2   Tbsp. panko (Japanese-style bread crumbs)
Kosher salt and freshly ground black pepper

2   boneless New York strip steaks, each 1 ¼ to 1 ½ in. thick (10 to 12 oz. each)
3   heirloom tomatoes, sliced
2   Tbsp. extra-virgin olive oil

1   Prepare an outdoor grill or heat a stovetop grill pan over medium-high heat.

2   In a food processor, pulse parsley and shallots until coarsely chopped. Add butter and pulse until blended together. Add bread crumbs and pulse about five times to combine. Transfer to a bowl; season with salt and pepper.

3   Season steaks with salt and pepper. Grill 5 to 6 minutes per side or until an instant-read thermometer reads 135°F to 140°F for medium-rare. Spread 1 tablespoon herb butter on each steak to slightly melt. (Reserve remainder for another use.) Let steaks rest, loosely covered with foil, 5 to 8 minutes.

4   Drizzle tomatoes with oil and season with salt and pepper to taste. Cut steaks on the diagonal and serve with tomatoes.

Each serving About 452 calories, 35 g protein, 5 g carbohydrate, 32 g total fat (12 g saturated), 1 g fiber, 132 mg cholesterol, 197 mg sodium.

Rocco DiSpirito's Cotechino with Lentils (Pork Tenderloin with Lentils)

Total time 55 minutes

Makes 4 servings

½ c. small green lentils, such as du Puy lentils
Olive oil cooking spray
1 piece pork tenderloin (20 oz.), trimmed of visible fat
Salt

Freshly ground black pepper
½ c. minced leeks
1 carrot, chopped
2 oz. dry-cured Italian salami, such as sopressata, minced
1 small celery root, peeled and finely chopped

1 qt. fat-free, reduced-sodium chicken broth, such as Swanson's
½ tsp. chopped fresh thyme leaves

1 Place lentils in a large bowl, cover with *water*, and soak overnight in the refrigerator.

2 Preheat oven to 325°F.

3 Coat a large nonstick ovenproof skillet or Dutch oven with 8 seconds of cooking spray and place over medium-high heat. Season pork with salt and pepper, place in pan, and brown evenly on all sides, about 2 minutes per side. Remove pork from pan to a plate and add lentils, leeks, carrot, salami, and celery root to pan. Pour in broth and bring to a boil. Reduce heat and simmer gently 5 minutes. Add pork to pan, cover, and place in oven. Cook until pork is just cooked through, 10 to 15 minutes. Remove pork and place on a wire rack to rest.

4 Return pan to stovetop and place over medium heat; continue to cook lentils until they are tender, about 15 minutes. Most of the broth will be absorbed, and you should be left with a tender lentil stew. Add thyme and season with salt and pepper. Place pork back in pan and simmer 2 minutes.

5 Divide stew among four bowls. Slice pork ½ inch thick and place over lentils.

Each serving About 329 calories, 41 g protein, 20 g carbohydrate, 9 g total fat (3 g saturated), 5 g fiber, 105 mg cholesterol, 978 mg sodium.

If the lentils haven't become tender before the liquid has been absorbed, add about ½ cup water and continue to simmer until they are done.

Bobby Flay's Red Curry–Marinated Skirt Steak Fajitas plus Pickled Peppers and Avocado Crema

Total time 50 minutes plus marinating

Makes 8 main-dish servings

2 Tbsp. red curry paste

¼ c. plus 2 Tbsp. canola oil

5 Tbsp. fresh lime juice
  (from about 3 limes)

2 lb. beef skirt steak,
  cut crosswise in thirds

¼ c. clover honey

1¼ tsp. kosher salt

¾ tsp. freshly ground
  black pepper

2 Vidalia or other sweet onions
  (1 lb. each),
  cut into ¼-in.-thick slices

1 Tbsp. steak rub seasoning

2 Tbsp. barbecue sauce

16 flour tortillas
  (6 in. in diameter)

Pickled Roasted Peppers
  (see recipe on page 113)

Avocado Crema (see recipe
  on page 112)

Fresh cilantro leaves,
  for garnish

1 In a food processor, puree curry paste, ¼ cup oil, and 2 tablespoons lime juice until smooth. In a large baking dish, rub mixture all over steak to coat. Cover with plastic wrap and refrigerate at least 4 hours or up to 12 hours.

2 In a small bowl, whisk honey and remaining 3 tablespoons lime juice.

3 Prepare an outdoor grill for direct grilling on high heat or heat a cast-iron grill pan on range over high heat. Remove steak from marinade and sprinkle with ¾ teaspoon salt and ½ teaspoon pepper. Grill steak 10 minutes for medium-rare (140°F on an instant-read thermometer) or until slightly charred on both sides, turning over once; transfer to a cutting board and let rest 10 minutes.

4 Reduce grill or range heat to medium.

5 Brush onion slices with remaining 2 tablespoons oil to coat and sprinkle with ½ teaspoon salt and ¼ teaspoon pepper. Sprinkle steak rub on one side of onion slices and place, rubbed side down, on hot grill grate; grill 2 minutes or until light golden brown. Turn slices over; brush with barbecue sauce. Grill 4 minutes or until just cooked through. Transfer to a medium bowl and separate into rings.

(continued on page 112)

6 Wrap tortillas in foil. Grill packet 5 minutes or until tortillas are warm.

7 Thinly slice steak across grain. Place slices on a large serving platter; immediately drizzle with honey-lime dressing. Lay warm tortillas on a flat surface and arrange a few slices of beef down center of each. Top with onion slices, pickled roasted peppers, a dollop of avocado crema, and some cilantro. Roll, and eat.

Each serving without crema or peppers About 510 calories, 29 g protein, 53 g carbohydrate, 20 g total fat (6 g saturated), 4 g fiber, 51 mg cholesterol, 795 mg sodium.

Bobby Flay's Avocado Crema

Total time 10 minutes   **Makes 1½ cups**

2 ripe Hass avocados, peeled, pitted, and chopped	**¼** tsp. kosher salt
2 Tbsp. fresh lime juice	**⅛** tsp. freshly ground black pepper
1 tsp. honey	
½ c. fresh cilantro leaves, chopped	

1 In a blender, combine avocados, lime juice, honey, and ¼ *cup water*; puree until smooth (if necessary, add *1 to 2 tablespoons water* to loosen mixture for pureeing).

2 Add cilantro, salt, and pepper; puree just until incorporated. Serve immediately.

Each tablespoon About 20 calories, 0 g protein, 1 g carbohydrate, 2 g total fat (0 g saturated), 1 g fiber, 0 mg cholesterol, 20 mg sodium.

Bobby Flay's
Pickled Roasted Peppers

Total time 1 hour 20 minutes plus cooling and pickling   **Makes 3⅓ cups**

2	medium red peppers	½	c. white wine vinegar
2	medium yellow peppers	½	c. cider vinegar
2	tsp. canola oil	1	garlic clove, thinly sliced
¼	tsp. plus 1 Tbsp. kosher salt	2	Tbsp. sugar
⅛	tsp. freshly ground	2	Tbsp. finely chopped fresh
	black pepper		oregano leaves

1   Preheat oven to 400°F.

2   On a jelly-roll pan, brush red and yellow peppers with oil and sprinkle with ¼ teaspoon salt and ⅛ teaspoon black pepper. Roast, turning occasionally, 30 minutes or until charred on all sides. Transfer to a bowl, cover with plastic wrap, and let stand 15 minutes.

3   Meanwhile, in a 1½-quart saucepan, combine vinegars, *½ cup water*, garlic, sugar, and 1 tablespoon salt. Bring to a boil over high heat, stirring. Boil 1 minute. Remove from heat; let cool.

4   Peel skin from peppers and discard; remove and discard stems and seeds. Thinly slice peppers and transfer to a medium bowl.

5   Stir in oregano and vinegar mixture. Cover and refrigerate at least 4 hours or up to 2 days.

Each ⅓ cup About 15 calories, 0 g protein, 4 g carbohydrate, 0 g total fat, 1 g fiber, 0 mg cholesterol, 50 mg sodium.

Bobby Flay loves hosting parties and he has a foolproof method for keeping things organized: "I'm a big 'list person.' I make one for shopping and one for prioritizing—from what can be done ahead of time to what can be left for the end, right before the guests arrive."

Stephanie Izard's
Lamb Tacos with Herbed Yogurt & Heirloom Tomatoes

Total time 30 minutes

Makes 4 servings

Tomatoes
1 ½ lb. heirloom tomatoes, diced
1 Tbsp. balsamic vinegar
1 Tbsp. extra-virgin olive oil
½ tsp. kosher salt
¼ tsp. freshly ground
   black pepper

Herbed yogurt
1 c. plain Greek yogurt
¼ c. chopped fresh herbs
   (cilantro, dill, or parsley)

½ tsp. kosher salt
¼ tsp. freshly ground
   black pepper

Lamb
1 ¼ lb. ground lamb
4 tsp. Dijon mustard
4 tsp. Worcestershire sauce
2 tsp. garam masala
   (Indian spice blend available
   at supermarkets)
¾ tsp. kosher salt

½ tsp. freshly ground
   black pepper
¼ tsp. crushed red pepper
   flakes
1 Tbsp. extra-virgin olive oil
12 corn tortillas, warmed
1 ½ c. shredded romaine lettuce

1   Prepare tomatoes: In a medium bowl, combine all ingredients.

2   Prepare herbed yogurt: In a food processor, blend all ingredients until mixture turns pale green. Scrape into a small bowl.

3   Prepare lamb: In a large bowl, combine lamb, mustard, Worcestershire sauce, garam masala, salt, black pepper, and red pepper flakes and stir until blended. Heat a large, heavy skillet over medium-high heat. Add oil and swirl to coat skillet. Add lamb mixture and cook, stirring frequently to break it up, until browned, about 6 minutes. Pour off fat.

4   Spread tortillas with herbed yogurt and top with lamb, tomatoes, and lettuce.

Each serving About 650 calories, 36 g protein, 45 g carbohydrate, 37 g total fat (15 g saturated), 8 g fiber, 113 mg cholesterol, 1,168 mg sodium.

Christina Tosi's Cornbake (recipe on page 120)

Side Dishes

Even celebrity chefs have to make side dishes to complement the main event. John Besh whips up some delicious roasted vegetables and Sara Moulton makes a Green Tomato Gratin that just might steal the spotlight. Never thought much of lima beans? Try Alice Waters' Lima Beans and you'll surely have a new outlook.

Sara Moulton's Green Tomato Gratin

Total time 30 minutes

Makes 8 servings

2 lb. green tomatoes (about 8), sliced ⅓ in. thick

Salt

3 Tbsp. extra-virgin olive oil, plus more for baking dish

2 garlic cloves, minced

1 tsp. red pepper flakes

18 butter-flavored crackers (such as Ritz), crushed

2 oz. finely grated Parmesan (about ½ c.)

2 Tbsp. chopped fresh marjoram

1 Preheat oven to 425°F. Sprinkle tomatoes liberally with salt and let drain in a colander for 15 minutes. Transfer to paper towels and gently pat dry. While tomatoes are draining, in a small bowl, combine oil, garlic, and red pepper flakes. Place tomatoes in a single layer in an oiled 9" by 13" baking dish. Drizzle with garlic oil.

2 In a small bowl, mix remaining ingredients. Sprinkle over tomatoes. Bake in upper third of oven until tops are browned, 12 to 15 minutes.

Each serving About 134 calories, 5 g protein, 11 g carbohydrate, 9 g total fat (2 g saturated), 2 g fiber, 6 mg cholesterol, 405 mg sodium.

Christina Tosi's Cornbake

Total time 50 minutes

Makes 8 servings

1 ⅓ c. all-purpose flour
1   c. cornmeal
3   Tbsp. granulated sugar
3   Tbsp. light brown sugar
1   Tbsp. baking powder
1   Tbsp. fine salt
1   tsp. baking soda

1   can (14 oz.) cream-style corn
1 ½ c. sour cream
1   egg plus 3 yolks, lightly
    beaten
¼   c. honey, plus more for
    drizzling
2   Tbsp. buttermilk

1   c. fresh or frozen corn kernels
½   c. (1 stick) unsalted butter,
    melted
2   Tbsp. shortening, melted,
    plus more for skillet
Coarse sea salt (such as Maldon)

1   Preheat oven to 400°F. In a large bowl, combine first seven ingredients.

2   In a medium bowl, combine cream-style corn, sour cream, egg, yolks, honey, and buttermilk. Stir in corn kernels, butter, and shortening.

3   Pour wet ingredients into dry ingredients; mix. Pour batter into a greased 10-inch cast-iron skillet. Bake until golden brown, about 30 minutes. Drizzle with honey and sprinkle with sea salt.

Each serving About 494 calories, 8 g protein, 63 g carbohydrate, 25 g total fat (13 g saturated), 2 g fiber, 142 mg cholesterol, 1,406 mg sodium.

Christina Tosi notes the incredible versatility of this sweet-and-savory wonder: "I also love it after dinner, with a scoop of ice cream."

John Besh's Roasted Root Vegetables with Chestnuts & Quince

Total time 1 hour 30 minutes

Makes 8 servings

Olive oil cooking spray

3 each small red and golden beets without tops (1 lb. total), peeled, cut into ½-in.-thick wedges

2 quince, quartered lengthwise, core and seeds removed, peeled, each quarter cut into thirds

4 medium white turnips without tops (1 lb.), peeled, cut into ½-in. wedges

¾ lb. each carrots and parsnips, peeled, quartered lengthwise, each cut into 3 or 4 pieces

1 large sweet onion (¾ lb.), halved, cut through root end into ½-in.-thick wedges

¼ c. small fresh sage leaves

1 Tbsp. fresh rosemary leaves

3 Tbsp. extra-virgin olive oil

1½ tsp. kosher salt, plus more to taste

½ tsp. freshly ground black pepper, plus more to taste

1½ c. roasted, peeled chestnuts

1 Tbsp. fresh thyme leaves

1 Preheat oven to 450°F. Spray a large roasting pan with cooking spray. Add all ingredients to roasting pan except chestnuts and thyme. Toss until everything is lightly coated with oil.

2 Roast 50 minutes, tossing vegetables every 15 minutes. Stir in chestnuts and continue to roast 10 minutes or until vegetables are tender. Stir in thyme. Adjust salt and pepper, if needed.

Each serving About 220 calories, 3 g protein, 39 g carbohydrate, 7 g total fat (1 g saturated), 7 g fiber, 0 mg cholesterol, 457 mg sodium.

Alice Waters' Lima Beans

Total time 50 minutes

3   lb. "Christmas" lima beans, shelled (about 3 c.)
2 to 3 Tbsp. olive oil, plus more for drizzling

1   tsp. salt, plus more for seasoning
1   bay leaf

3 to 4 fresh sage leaves, or 1 sprig fresh rosemary or thyme
Freshly ground black pepper

1   In a large pot, add beans and enough *water* to cover by 2 inches. Add oil, 1 teaspoon salt, bay leaf, and herb leaves or sprig. Bring bean mixture to a boil, reduce heat to a simmer, and cook gently until beans are tender throughout, 30 to 45 minutes (sample several beans to ensure doneness). Turn off heat and let beans cool in broth.

2   When ready to serve, in same pot, gently reheat beans over medium heat. Pour off most broth (save it for soup or some other use, if desired). Season with salt and pepper and top with a drizzle of olive oil.

Each serving About 112 calories, 4 g protein, 14 g carbohydrate, 4 g total fat (1 g saturated), 3 g fiber, 0 mg cholesterol, 112 mg sodium.

What Music Do You Listen to While You Cook?

"[The Sex Pistols] keep me moving when I'm cooking for lots of people."
—Curtis Stone, host of *Top Chef Masters* and *Around the World in 80 Plates*

"I get in the groove with classic rock, like Bon Jovi—I'm a Jersey guy!"
—Buddy Valastro, star of *Cake Boss*

"I know [husband and co-host] Gabriele [Corcos] wants to cook alone when he plays Metallica. I can't tolerate it. When I want the kitchen to myself, I'll put on 'I Will Survive.'"
—Debi Mazar, host of *Extra Virgin*

"When I cook, I listen to old rock 'n' roll, like Elton John and Pink Floyd. But I love Lady Gaga."
—Wolfgang Puck, owner of Spago restaurants

Emeril Lagasse's
Provençal-Style Stuffed Zucchini

Total time 1 hour 30 minutes

Makes 8 servings

2 c. diced French baguette or other crusty bread (½-in. cubes), preferably day-old
¼ c. finely grated Parmesan
¼ c. packed fresh flat-leaf parsley leaves
1 Tbsp. finely chopped garlic

⅝ tsp. salt, plus more to taste
¼ tsp. freshly ground black pepper, plus more to taste
3 Tbsp. extra-virgin olive oil
8 small zucchini (each about 7 in. long and 1¼ to 1½ in. wide)

4 oz. fresh lean mild pork sausage, casings removed
¾ c. finely chopped onion
1 c. peeled, seeded, and chopped tomatoes (from about 2 medium)

1 In a food processor with knife blade attached, pulse bread into an even mix of fine and coarse crumbs. Add Parmesan, parsley, half of garlic, ¼ teaspoon salt, and ⅛ teaspoon pepper; process until evenly mixed. Reserve 2 tablespoons bread-crumb mixture for filling. Mix 1½ tablespoons oil into remaining bread crumbs and set aside. (Or, use store-bought fine fresh crumbs: Combine ¾ cup bread crumbs with ¼ cup finely grated Parmesan, 1 tablespoon finely chopped parsley, ½ teaspoon finely chopped garlic, ¾ teaspoon salt, and ⅛ teaspoon freshly ground black pepper. Set aside 2 tablespoons mixture, and mix 1½ tablespoons oil into remainder.)

2 On a flat work surface, with a sharp knife, slice off top length-wise quarter of each zucchini (reserve quarters for another use). Cut a sliver off bottom to help keep it stable. With a spoon or melon baller, scoop pulp from zucchini, leaving a ¼-inch-thick shell. Cut pulp into ¼-inch cubes; set aside. Sprinkle inside of shells with ¼ teaspoon salt; place, hollow side down, on paper towels to drain.

3 Make filling: In a 12-inch skillet, heat 1 tablespoon oil over medium heat. Add sausage and cook 6 minutes or until golden brown; break into small pieces with a spoon. Add onion and cook 4 minutes or until soft. Add cubed pulp and cook 2 minutes. Add tomatoes and remaining garlic and cook, stirring, 2 minutes or until moisture has evaporated and filling comes together. Remove skillet from heat; stir in reserved 2 tablespoons bread-crumb mixture and add salt and pepper if necessary.

4 Preheat oven to 350°F. Rub outsides of zucchini with remaining oil and sprinkle with ⅛ teaspoon each salt and pepper. Turn zucchini hollow side up and lightly pat insides with paper towels. With a small spoon, fill zucchini with warm filling. Top with remaining bread crumbs.

5 Place zucchini in a shallow baking dish and bake 30 minutes or until golden and crisp on top.

Each serving About 160 calories, 6 g protein, 13 g carbohydrate, 9 g total fat (2 g saturated), 2 g fiber, 13 mg cholesterol, 385 mg sodium.

Beekman Boys'
Leek & Potato Gratin

Total time 1 hour 15 minutes   Makes 12 servings

3	lb. small potatoes (such as red or Yukon gold), sliced ⅛ in. thick
2	tablespoons unsalted butter, plus more for buttering dish

10	medium leeks, white and light-green parts only, halved lengthwise and cut crosswise into 1-in. pieces (washed thoroughly)

4	garlic cloves, thinly sliced
2	c. heavy cream
1	c. milk
1½	tsp. salt
¼	c. chopped fresh flat-leaf parsley, for garnish

1   Preheat oven to 375°F. In a large pot of *salted boiling water*, parboil potatoes 5 minutes. Drain potatoes well and set aside.

2   In a large skillet, heat butter over medium heat. Sauté leeks and garlic until leeks are tender, about 7 minutes. Set aside.

3   In a buttered 9" by 13" baking dish, arrange half of reserved potatoes in an overlapping pattern. Pour 1 cup cream and ½ cup milk over top and sprinkle with 1 teaspoon salt. Top with reserved leeks and arrange remaining potatoes. Pour remaining cream and milk over potatoes and sprinkle with ½ teaspoon salt. Bake until potatoes are tender, top of gratin is golden brown, and most of cream and milk have been absorbed, about 45 minutes. Garnish with parsley.

Each serving About 290 calories, 5 g protein, 30 g carbohydrate, 18 g total fat (11 g saturated), 3 g fiber, 62 mg cholesterol, 290 mg sodium.

"There's nothing like the flavor of a freshly dug potato. In this luscious fall gratin, potatoes get the royal treatment."

—Beekman Boys

Guy Fieri's Black-Eyed Basmati Salad

Total time 30 minutes

Makes 8 servings

½ c. basmati rice
1 tsp. minced garlic
¼ c. apple cider vinegar
3 Tbsp. whole-grain
   Dijon mustard
2 Tbsp. extra-virgin olive oil

1 Tbsp. honey
1 Tbsp. minced shallot
1 Tbsp. chopped fresh cilantro
1 can (15½ oz.) black-eyed
   peas, rinsed and drained
½ cup diced red bell pepper

⅓ c. pimiento-stuffed
   Spanish olives, sliced
¼ c. diced red onion
1 tsp. freshly ground
   black pepper

1   In a small saucepan, combine rice, *1 cup water*, and garlic. Bring to a boil, cover pan, and simmer over low heat 15 minutes or until water is absorbed and rice is just tender. Let cool. Fluff with a fork.

2   In a large bowl, combine vinegar, mustard, oil, honey, shallot, and cilantro and whisk until combined. Add rice and remaining ingredients and toss until evenly dressed. Salad can be refrigerated up to 2 hours before serving.

Each serving About 132 calories, 4 g protein, 21 g carbohydrate, 5 g total fat (1 g saturated), 3 g fiber, 0 mg cholesterol, 337 mg sodium.

Vinegars add intense flavor to many dishes and each variety is unique. Guy Fieri says, "I'm a vinegar junkie—I always have at least five types on hand."

John Besh's Angel Biscuits

Total time 45 minutes plus rising

Makes 12 servings

1 package active dry yeast	¼ c. sugar	1 c. (2 sticks) unsalted butter
5 c. all-purpose flour, plus ½ c. more for surface	2 Tbsp. baking powder	2 c. buttermilk
	1½ tsp. salt	

1   In a small bowl, dissolve yeast in *¼ cup warm water* (100°F to 110°F) and set aside. In a large bowl, sift together 5 cups flour, sugar, baking powder, and salt. Using a pastry blender, cut butter into flour mixture. Add buttermilk and reserved yeast mixture and mix well to form a light, fairly wet dough.

2   Sprinkle ¼ cup flour on a work surface. Divide dough in half and roll out one piece into a ½-inch-thick 9" by 18" rectangle. Fold dough lengthwise in thirds to create a triple-layered 3" by 18" rectangle. Cut into six 3-inch squares. Repeat with remaining flour and dough for a total of 12 biscuits. Place biscuits, just touching, on a nonstick baking sheet; cover loosely with plastic wrap and refrigerate overnight to rise.

3   Preheat oven to 400°F. Meanwhile, remove biscuits from refrigerator and let sit 10 minutes. Bake biscuits until golden brown, 15 to 20 minutes.

Each serving About 384 calories, 8 g protein, 52 g carbohydrate, 16 g total fat (10 g saturated), 2 g fiber, 42 mg cholesterol, 612 mg sodium.

"I want people to make the food, not worry too much about ingredients or complicated techniques. I think it's important to put good, fresh, healthy food on the table."

—John Besh

Martha Stewart's Gingerbread Cookies plus Royal Icing (recipe on page 144

Desserts

Get ready for the grand finale—luscious desserts from your favorite chefs. Just try to resist such creations as Marcus Samuelsson's Whiskey Fudge or Todd English's Apple Crepes. For the holidays, bake up some of Martha Stewart's famous Gingerbread Cookies plus Royal Icing or inspire awe with the Beekman Boys' Lemon Pudding Cake.

Marcus Samuelsson's Whiskey Fudge

Total time 25 minutes plus setting

Makes 60 pieces

Olive oil cooking spray
1½ c. heavy cream
¼ c. whiskey, preferably Jack Daniel's

1⅓ c. sugar
1 lb. bittersweet or semisweet chocolate, finely chopped

1 Tbsp. flaked sea salt (such as Maldon)
½ c. finely chopped toasted macadamia nuts or pecans

1 Lightly spray an 11" by 7" or 8-inch square baking pan with cooking spray. Line pan with plastic wrap, letting wrap extend several inches above the sides. Carefully smooth out any wrinkles in plastic. Set aside.

2 In a small saucepan, combine cream and whiskey and heat over low heat.

3 Meanwhile, in a heavy-bottomed 3-quart saucepan, combine sugar and ⅓ *cup water* and cook over high heat, without stirring, until sugar dissolves. Continue to boil sugar syrup until it turns golden amber, about 7 minutes. Immediately remove from heat. Slowly add hot cream mixture in several batches, stirring with a heat-resistant rubber spatula until blended (the mixture will bubble up high).

4 Attach a candy thermometer to side of saucepan and continue to cook mixture over medium heat until it reaches 230°F on the thermometer, 5 to 7 minutes. Remove saucepan from heat and let mixture cool to 150°F, about 10 minutes. Gently stir in chocolate and salt until chocolate is melted and mixture is smooth.

5 Pour mixture into prepared pan and spread into an even layer with a metal spatula. Let stand at room temperature until bottom of pan is no longer warm, then refrigerate, covered with plastic wrap touching surface of fudge, until it sets, about 3 hours.

6 To serve, use plastic wrap to lift fudge from pan and invert it onto a cutting board. Peel off plastic and cut fudge crosswise into 1-inch strips. Cut each strip into 1-inch squares. Roll edges of squares in nuts.

Each serving About 83 calories, 1 g protein, 9 g carbohydrate, 6 g total fat (3 g saturated), 1 g fiber, 8 mg cholesterol, 56 mg sodium.

Chocolate Tips from Chocolatier Jacques Torres

1 Use fresh chocolate. Yes, there is such a thing! In fact, Jacques Torres feels so strongly about this point that he built chocolate-making facilities in his factory. Now, he can start from the cacao beans and take them from the roasting process to the final bar stage. (He had previously bought chocolate from high-quality purveyors and still does, as do most chocolatiers.) Obviously, we can't make our own chocolate, but we can buy bars just before using them and always check the "best before" date on the package.

2 Keep it simple. Jacques Torres is best known for his simplest creations: chocolate-covered Cheerios, nut barks, cornflake clusters. If you start with delicious, high-quality chocolate, you don't need to add much to it to make it even better.

3 Make edible art! Jacques Torres is famous for his fanciful creations and he encourages whimsical decorating at home too. He uses perfect parchment-paper cornets to pipe his chocolate and paintbrushes for extra embellishments. Try that, or use a resealable plastic bag with a hole cut out of one corner to decorate with chocolate.

Mark Bittman's
Stone Fruit Patchwork Bake

Total time 1 hour

Makes 6-8 servings

½ c. (1 stick) cold unsalted butter, cut into about 8 pieces, more for dish	½ tsp. salt	1 c. cherries, stones in or pitted
1½ c. all-purpose flour, more for rolling	¾ c. plus 2 tablespoons sugar	1 Tbsp. freshly squeezed lemon juice
	3 lb. peaches, seeded and sliced (about 5 large)	

1 Heat oven to 400°F and butter a 9" by 13" or similar-size baking dish; set aside. In a food processor, combine 1 cup plus 2 tablespoons flour, salt, and 1 tablespoon sugar; pulse once or twice. Add butter and process until butter and flour are blended and mixture looks like coarse cornmeal, about 15 to 20 seconds. Slowly add *¼ cup ice water* through feed tube and process until just combined. Form dough into flat disk, wrap in plastic, and freeze for 10 minutes or refrigerate for at least 30 minutes. (You can refrigerate dough for up to a couple of days, or freeze it, tightly wrapped, for up to a couple of weeks.)

2 Meanwhile, in a large bowl, toss fruit with remaining flour, ¾ cup sugar, and lemon juice; place in baking dish.

3 Put dough on a floured board or countertop and sprinkle with more flour. Roll dough into 12-inch round, adding flour and rotating dough as needed. Cut dough into 3-inch-wide strips, then cut again crosswise into 4-inch-long pieces. Scatter pieces over fruit in overlapping patchwork pattern.

4 Brush top of dough lightly with *water* and sprinkle with remaining tablespoon sugar. Transfer to oven and bake until top is golden brown and juices bubble, 35 to 45 minutes. Transfer to a wire rack to cool; serve warm or at room temperature.

Each serving About 396 calories, 5 g protein, 63 g carbohydrate, 16 g total fat (9 g saturated), 3 g fiber, 39 mg cholesterol, 170 mg sodium.

Todd English's Apple Crepes

Total time 30 minutes

Makes 8 servings

6   Tbsp. unsalted butter
4   large Gala apples, peeled,
     cored, and sliced
¾   c. sugar

1   tsp. ground cinnamon
1½   tsp. salt
6   large eggs
1   c. milk

1   c. all-purpose flour, sifted
2   Tbsp. vegetable oil
½   c. mascarpone

1   In a large pan melt butter over high heat. Add apples, ½ cup sugar, cinnamon, and ½ teaspoon salt, and sauté 5 minutes. Set aside.

2   In a medium bowl, whisk eggs and milk. Add flour and remaining ¼ cup sugar and 1 teaspoon salt; whisk until smooth. Heat a 6-inch nonstick pan over high heat. Brush pan with some oil and coat with ¼ cup batter. Cook crepe until golden, about 1 minute; flip and cook 30 seconds. Repeat with remaining batter, brushing pan with oil between crepes.

3   Fill each crepe with ¼ cup apples, fold in half, and top with 1 tablespoon mascarpone.

Each serving About 488 calories, 10 g protein, 48 g carbohydrate, 30 g total fat (13 g saturated), 3 g fiber, 200 mg cholesterol, 375 mg sodium.

Beekman Boys' Lemon Pudding Cake

Total time 55 minutes

1 Tbsp. grated lemon zest
   (from about 2 lemons)
⅔ c. plus 1 Tbsp. sugar
¼ c. all-purpose flour

1 c. milk
⅓ c. fresh lemon juice
   (from about 2 lemons)
¼ c. heavy cream

3 Tbsp. unsalted butter, melted
   and cooled
3 large eggs, separated
¼ tsp. salt

1   Preheat oven to 350°F. Grease an 8-inch square baking dish.
Put a kettle of *water* on to boil.

2   In a large bowl, combine lemon zest and ⅔ cup sugar, mashing
zest into sugar. Whisk in flour, milk, lemon juice, cream, butter, and
egg yolks until smooth.

3   In a separate bowl, beat egg whites with salt until foamy. Beat
in remaining 1 tablespoon sugar until soft peaks form. Stir about
one-fourth of egg whites into flour mixture to lighten slightly, and
then gently fold in remaining egg whites. Pour into baking dish.

4   Set baking dish in a larger pan. Set pan on a pulled-out oven
rack, and pour in *boiling water* to come halfway up sides of
baking dish. Bake 40 minutes or until top is golden brown and set.
Transfer pan to a rack to cool. Serve warm.

Each serving About 263 calories, 5 g protein, 32 g carbohydrate, 13 g total
fat(8 g saturated), 0 g fiber, 126 mg cholesterol, 155 mg sodium.

Make an orange pudding cake by swapping in ¼ cup orange juice,
2 tablespoons lemon juice, and 1 tablespoon grated orange zest for
the lemon. Or use Meyer lemons in place of regular lemons.

Ted Allen's Mixed-Berry Crumble plus Honey-Vanilla Ice Cream

Total time 1 hour 10 minutes   **Makes 10 servings**

1 pt. blackberries	¼ c. honey	½ c. (1 stick) unsalted butter
½ pt. raspberries	¾ c. all-purpose flour	**Honey-Vanilla Ice Cream**
½ pt. strawberries, hulled and sliced	½ c. rolled oats	(recipe on page 143)
	½ c. packed light brown sugar	

1   Preheat oven to 375°F. In a large bowl, mix berries. Drizzle with honey. Sprinkle with 4 tablespoons flour and toss. Transfer fruit to an 8-inch square baking dish.

2   In a large bowl, using a pastry blender or your fingers, combine remaining ½ cup flour, oats, brown sugar, and butter until mixture forms large, crumbly lumps. Sprinkle over berries. Bake until golden brown, 45 to 50 minutes. Serve with honey-vanilla ice cream.

Each serving without ice cream About 223 calories, 2 g protein, 33 g carbohydrate, 10 g total fat (6 g saturated), 3 g fiber, 24 mg cholesterol, 5 mg sodium.

"I'm all for a meal having elements of surprise, but I like to serve straightforward, seasonal food that doesn't rely on a lot of fussy components."

—Ted Allen

Ted Allen's
Honey-Vanilla Ice Cream

Total time 30 minutes plus chilling and freezing   **Makes 1 quart**

3	**c. heavy cream**	2 **vanilla beans, split**
1	**c. milk**	4 **large egg yolks**
½	**c. honey**	1 **Tbsp. vanilla extract**

1   In a medium saucepan, heat first four ingredients over medium heat until hot (don't let boil), about 5 minutes.

2   In a medium bowl, whisk egg yolks. Drizzle 1 cup hot cream mixture into yolks, whisking continuously. Pour back into saucepan and whisk over medium heat until custard thickens slightly, about 5 minutes. Pour through a fine-mesh strainer. Scrape vanilla seeds into custard. Add vanilla extract. Cover and chill, about 1 hour.

3   Following directions on your ice-cream maker, churn custard. Transfer into airtight containers; freeze for at least 2 more hours.

Each serving About 340 calories, 3 g protein, 17 g carbohydrate, 29 g total fat (18 g saturated), 0 g fiber, 175 mg cholesterol, 42 mg sodium.

Martha Stewart's
Gingerbread Cookies plus Royal Icing

Total time 55 minutes plus chilling and cooling

Makes 2 dozen cookies

3½ c. all-purpose flour, plus
    additional for dusting
1½ tsp. baking soda
¼ tsp. salt
1¼ tsp. ground cinnamon
1¼ tsp. ground ginger

1¼ tsp. ground allspice
¼ tsp. ground cloves
1 c. (2 sticks) unsalted butter,
    softened
¾ c. granulated sugar
¾ c. packed dark brown sugar

1 Tbsp. plus 1 tsp. peeled
    and grated fresh ginger
1 large egg
¼ c. unsulfured molasses
Royal Icing (recipe on opposite
    page; optional)

1   In a large bowl, using a wire whisk, mix flour, baking soda, salt, cinnamon, ground ginger, allspice, and cloves; set aside.

2   In a large bowl, with mixer on low speed, beat butter, sugars, and fresh ginger until combined. Increase speed to medium; beat until light and fluffy, 2 to 3 minutes, occasionally scraping bowl with rubber spatula. Add egg and molasses and beat until blended. With mixer on low speed, gradually add flour mixture, beating until just incorporated. Transfer dough to a clean work surface. Divide dough in half, and flatten each half into a disk; wrap disks in plastic wrap. Refrigerate at least 1 hour or overnight.

3   Arrange two racks in upper and lower thirds of oven. Preheat oven to 350°F. Line two large cookie sheets with parchment paper; set aside. Remove dough from refrigerator and let stand until slightly softened. (This will help keep dough from cracking when rolled.) On large piece of parchment paper lightly dusted with flour, with a floured rolling pin, roll dough to about ¼-inch thickness. To prevent sticking while rolling, occasionally run a large metal offset spatula under dough, and sprinkle with more flour. Place parchment paper and dough on another cookie sheet; freeze until very firm, about 15 minutes.

4   Remove dough from freezer; working quickly, with floured large cookie cutters, cut out desired shapes. (If dough begins to soften too much, return to freezer for a few minutes.) With a wide metal spatula, transfer cutouts to prepared baking sheets; chill until firm, about 15 minutes.

5 Bake cookies until crisp but not darkened, 12 to 15 minutes, rotating sheets between upper and lower racks halfway through baking. Transfer cookies, on parchment, to wire rack to cool completely. Decorate as desired with royal icing, if using. Store cookies in an airtight container at room temperature for up to 5 days.

Each cookie without icing About 200 calories, 2 g protein, 30 g carbohydrate, 8 g total fat (5 g saturated), 1 g fiber, 29 mg cholesterol, 110 mg sodium.

Martha Stewart's Royal Icing

Total time 5 minutes   **Makes ¾ cup**

2 c. confectioners' sugar **2 Tbsp. meringue powder**	**Assorted food colorings, optional**

1 In a bowl, with mixer at low speed, beat confectioners' sugar, meringue powder, and *3 tablespoons water* until blended. Scrape side of bowl with a rubber spatula. Increase speed to medium; beat until soft peaks form, about 10 minutes. Icing should be stiff enough to hold its shape when piped. Thin with more *water*, if needed.

2 Tint icing by gently stirring in food colorings as desired; keep surface covered with plastic wrap to prevent drying out.

Each tablespoon About 85 calories, 2 g protein, 20 g carbohydrate, 0 g total fat, 0 g fiber, 0 mg cholesterol, 0 mg sodium.

"As cutout cookies, [these] have a good color and hold their shape nicely. And the gingerbread has a real bite to it."

—Martha Stewart

Carla Hall's Apple Bread Pudding

Total time 1 hour 30 minutes   **Makes 12 servings**

5 Tbsp. unsalted butter (2 Tbsp. melted)	**3 large Granny Smith apples,** peeled, cut into ½-in. cubes	**¼ tsp. kosher salt**
1 lb. stale challah or brioche bread, cut into 1-in. cubes (or let a fresh cubed loaf stand overnight on a large baking sheet)	**2 Tbsp. plus 1 c. granulated sugar**	**3 c. milk**
	4 large eggs	**2 c. heavy cream**
	2 large egg yolks	**2 tsp. vanilla extract**
	1 tsp. ground cinnamon	**¾ c. honey**
		1 fresh sage sprig
		Whipped cream, optional

1   Preheat oven to 350°F. Butter a 2½-quart baking dish with 1 tablespoon butter.

2   On a large rimmed baking sheet, toss bread cubes with 2 tablespoons melted butter; spread out. Bake 10 minutes or until lightly toasted; let cool.

3   In a large skillet, melt remaining butter over medium-high heat. Add apples and 2 tablespoons sugar. Reduce heat to medium and cook, stirring frequently, 5 minutes or until apples are tender.

4   In a large bowl, whisk eggs, egg yolks, cinnamon, salt, and remaining 1 cup sugar until thoroughly blended. Add milk, cream, and vanilla; whisk until well blended.

5   Place bread cubes in prepared baking dish. Scatter apples on top of bread. Pour egg mixture over top. Let stand 1 hour at room temperature, occasionally pressing bread into egg mixture.

6   Bake until edges of pudding are set, top is golden, and center jiggles slightly, 45 to 50 minutes. Let cool on a wire rack until warm, about 1 hour.

7   In a microwave-safe bowl, combine honey and sage. Microwave on High 1 minute or until honey is warm and flavors are melded. Remove sage and drizzle half of honey over pudding. Serve with remaining honey and whipped cream, if desired.

Each serving without whipped cream About 523 calories, 9 g protein, 66 g carbohydrate, 26 g total fat (15 g saturated), 2 g fiber, 186 mg cholesterol, 264 mg sodium.

"By using a bread that's already sweet, like a brioche or challah, you can cut down on the amount of sugar you need for the dish," says Hall. Another reason to love bread pudding: The longer it sits, the better it tastes.

Beekman Boys'
Sour Cream–Sweet Potato Pie

Total time 1 hour 35 minutes plus chilling   **Makes 8 servings**

- 1 ¼ c. plus 2 Tbsp. all-purpose flour, plus more for dusting
- 1 Tbsp. sugar
- ¼ tsp. salt
- 4 Tbsp. cold unsalted butter, cut into ½-in. pieces; plus 3 Tbsp.

- 4 Tbsp. cold lard, cut into ½-in. pieces
- 1 c. packed light brown sugar
- ½ tsp. ground cinnamon
- ¼ tsp. grated nutmeg
- ¼ tsp. salt
- ½ c. milk

- ½ c. sour cream
- 3 large eggs
- 1 large egg yolk
- 1 tsp. pure vanilla extract
- 2 c. pureed cooked sweet potatoes (from about 1 ½ lb.)

Note: No lard in your kitchen? Substitute 4 tablespoons butter for a total of ½ cup (1 stick) in step 1.

1   In a food processor, pulse together 1 ¼ cups flour, sugar, and salt. Add cold butter and lard and pulse 10 times or until large pea-size lumps form. With motor running, gradually add *ice water* just until dough holds together when pinched between two fingers. Shape dough into a disk, wrap in plastic wrap, and refrigerate for at least 1 hour or up to 2 days.

2   On a lightly floured surface, roll out dough to a 12-inch round. Fit into a 9-inch deep-dish pie plate. Trim edges of dough, leaving a 1-inch overhang all around. Set aside dough scraps. Fold overhang over to form a high edge, then crimp dough.

3   To make decorative leaves: On a lightly floured surface, reroll leftover dough scraps to a ⅛-inch thickness. Using a leaf cookie cutter, press out 10 to 12 leaves. Using a sharp knife, score leaves to create veins. Moisten unscored side of each leaf with *water*, then arrange around pie edge, pressing gently to affix. Refrigerate crust to keep chilled.

To get a pie that isn't overly sweet, the Beekman Boys use two kinds of sweet potatoes: "Japanese sweet potatoes, which are a little drier in texture and mildly sweet, and deep-orange and garnet potatoes, which are moist and quite sweet," say the Beekman Boys.

4   Preheat oven to 350°F. Meanwhile, in a large bowl, whisk together brown sugar, 2 tablespoons flour, cinnamon, nutmeg, and salt until well combined. Whisk in milk, sour cream, eggs, egg yolk, and vanilla. Whisk in sweet potatoes. In a small saucepan over medium heat, melt remaining 3 tablespoons butter. Cook until butter foams; then continue until foam subsides and butter turns a rich brown. Immediately pour butter into sweet-potato mixture and whisk until incorporated.

5   Place pie plate on a rimmed baking sheet. Pour filling into crust. Bake until pie sets but center is still slightly wobbly, 50 to 60 minutes. Transfer to a wire rack to cool.

Each serving About 467 calories, 7 g protein, 61 g carbohydrate, 27 g total fat (15 g saturated), 3 g fiber, 133 mg cholesterol, 148 mg sodium.

David Guas' Pecan Pie

Total time 1 hour 20 minutes

Makes 8 servings

Crust

- 1 ⅓ c. all-purpose flour, plus more for dusting
- 1 Tbsp. sugar
- ½ tsp. salt
- ½ c. (1 stick) unsalted butter, cut into small cubes

Filling

- 1 large egg
- 5 large egg yolks
- ⅔ c. cane syrup
- ⅔ c. packed light brown sugar
- ½ c. heavy cream
- ¼ tsp. salt
- ½ c. (1 stick) unsalted butter, cut into small pieces
- 1 tsp. vanilla extract
- 1 ¾ c. pecan pieces

1 Prepare crust: In a food processor, pulse flour, sugar, and salt to combine. Add butter; pulse until pieces are the size of corn kernels. Sprinkle *4 tablespoons ice water* over mixture and pulse 6 times or until dough starts to hold together (if it's still dry, add another *1 tablespoon ice water*). Turn dough out on a work surface and form into a disk. Wrap in plastic wrap and chill 1 hour.

2 Preheat oven to 325°F. Unwrap dough. On a lightly floured surface, with a floured rolling pin, roll dough out to a 12-inch-diameter, ⅛-inch-thick round. Fold into quarters and transfer to a 9-inch pie plate. Unfold and mold into plate. Trim edges to a ¾-inch overhang. Turn edges under, crimp with fingers, and refrigerate.

3 Prepare filling: In a large bowl, whisk egg and egg yolks together. In a saucepan, combine cane syrup, sugar, cream, and salt until blended. Add butter and cook over medium heat until melted, then cook until mixture is hot but not bubbling, 1 minute longer. Gradually whisk syrup mixture into eggs until blended. Stir in vanilla.

4 Sprinkle pecan pieces over bottom of crust and pour filling on top. Bake until filling is set around edges but center jiggles slightly, 45 to 50 minutes. Cool on a wire rack 1 hour before slicing.

Each serving About 684 calories, 7 g protein, 56 g carbohydrate, 49 g total fat (21 g saturated), 3 g fiber, 220 mg cholesterol, 247 mg sodium.

Daisy Martinez's
Guava & Cheese Pastelillos

Total time 35 minutes plus cooling

Makes 8 turnovers

1   Tbsp. granulated sugar, for dusting surface
1   package frozen puff pastry (1 lb.), thawed

1   package (8 oz.) cream cheese, cut into 8 equal pieces
8   squares (1" by 1") guava paste (about 4 oz.)

1   egg, beaten with 1 tsp. water
¼   c. confectioners' sugar
1   tsp. milk
¼   tsp. vanilla extract

1   Preheat oven to 400°F. Sprinkle sugar on a work surface to prevent dough from sticking. Roll out each sheet of puff pastry to an 8-inch square. Using a pizza cutter or sharp knife, cut each sheet into 4 squares.

2   Make the turnovers: Set a pastry square in front of you with one corner pointing toward you. Place 1 piece cream cheese diagonally over center of bottom of square. Top with 1 piece guava paste. Brush edges of square with beaten egg.

3   Fold upper half of square over filling to make a neat triangle. Crimp edges with a fork. Repeat with remaining turnovers, placing them on a parchment-paper-lined baking sheet as you go. Bake 20 minutes or until golden brown and puffy.

4   While turnovers are baking, in a bowl, mix confectioners' sugar with milk and vanilla, stirring to dissolve any lumps. Set aside. Cool turnovers on a rack 10 to 15 minutes, then drizzle glaze over them. Serve warm or at room temperature.

Each turnover About 404 calories, 7 g protein, 37 g carbohydrate, 26 g total fat (10 g saturated), 2 g fiber, 55 mg cholesterol, 379 mg sodium.

Bobby Flay's
Mexican Chocolate Thumbprints

Total time 1 hour 45 minutes plus chilling and cooling

Makes about 5 dozen cookies

2 c. all-purpose flour	2 Tbsp. plus 1 tsp. vegetable oil	2 tsp. vanilla extract
1 tsp. ground cinnamon	1 c. (2 sticks) unsalted butter, softened	2 large egg whites, lightly beaten
½ tsp. salt	¾ c. granulated sugar	½ c. pecans, ground
6 Tbsp. Dutch-process cocoa powder	¼ c. packed light brown sugar	1 c. dulce de leche
1 tsp. espresso powder	2 large egg yolks	

1 In a large bowl, using a wire whisk, stir flour, cinnamon, and salt until blended. In a small bowl, using a rubber spatula, combine cocoa powder, espresso powder, and oil until mixture becomes smooth paste.

2 In another large bowl, with mixer on medium-high speed, beat butter and sugars until light and fluffy. Beat in egg yolks, one at a time, on medium speed until combined. Beat in vanilla, then cocoa mixture, until combined. Add flour mixture and beat on low speed just until dough comes together. Cover bowl with plastic wrap and refrigerate at least 20 minutes or up to 8 hours.

3 Preheat oven to 350°F. Line three cookie sheets with parchment paper.

4 Roll 2 teaspoons dough into a ball. Dip top of ball into egg whites, then pecans. Place on cookie sheet. Repeat with remaining dough, spacing balls 1½ inches apart. With thumb or back of spoon, make a deep indentation into center of each ball.

5 Bake, one sheet of cookies at a time, 9 minutes or until edges are set but centers are still soft. If necessary, make indentations again. Cool on pan on a wire rack 2 minutes. With a metal spatula, carefully transfer cookies to rack and cool completely. Store in an airtight container at room temperature up to 3 days.

6 To serve, fill centers of cookies with ½ teaspoon dulce de leche.

Each cookie About 85 calories, 1 g protein, 10 g carbohydrate, 5 g total fat (2 g saturated), 0 g fiber, 17 mg cholesterol, 30 mg sodium.

Metric Equivalents

The recipes in this book use the standard United States method for measuring liquid and dry or solid ingredients (teaspoons, tablespoons, and cups). The information in these charts is provided to help cooks outside the U.S. successfully use these recipes. All equivalents are approximate.

Metric Equivalents for Different Types of Ingredients

A standard cup measure of a dry or solid ingredient will vary in weight depending on the type of ingredient. A standard cup of liquid is the same volume for any type of liquid. Use the following chart when converting standard cup measures to grams (weight) or milliliters (volume).

Standard Cup	Fine Powder (e.g., flour)	Grain (e.g., rice)	Granular (e.g., sugar)	Liquid Solids (e.g., butter)	Liquid (e.g., milk)
1	140 g	150 g	190 g	200 g	240 ml
¾	105 g	113 g	143 g	150 g	180 ml
⅔	93 g	100 g	125 g	133 g	160 ml
½	70 g	75 g	95 g	100 g	120 ml
⅓	47 g	50 g	63 g	67 g	80 ml
¼	35 g	38 g	48 g	50 g	60 ml
⅛	18 g	19 g	24 g	25 g	30 ml

Useful Equivalents for Liquid Ingredients by Volume

¼ tsp	=						1 ml
½ tsp	=						2 ml
1 tsp	=						5 ml
3 tsp	=	1 tblsp	=	½ fl oz	=		15 ml
2 tblsp	=	⅛ cup	=	1 fl oz	=		30 ml
4 tblsp	=	¼ cup	=	2 fl oz	=		60 ml
5 ⅓ tblsp	=	⅓ cup	=	3 fl oz	=		80 ml
8 tblsp	=	½ cup	=	4 fl oz	=		120 ml
10 ⅔ tblsp	=	⅔ cup	=	5 fl oz	=		160 ml
12 tblsp	=	¾ cup	=	6 fl oz	=		180 ml
16 tblsp	=	1 cup	=	8 fl oz	=		240 ml
1 pt	=	2 cups	=	16 fl oz	=		480 ml
1 qt	=	4 cups	=	32 fl oz	=		960 ml
				33 fl oz	=		1000 ml

Useful Equivalents for Cooking / Oven Temperatures

	Fahrenheit	Celsius	Gas Mark
Freeze water	32° F	0° C	
Room temperature	68° F	20° C	
Boil water	212° F	100° C	
Bake	325° F	160° C	3
	350° F	180° C	4
	375° F	190° C	5
	400° F	200° C	6
	425° F	220° C	7
	450° F	230° C	8
Broil			Grill

Useful Equivalents for Dry Ingredients by Weight
(To convert ounces to grams, multiply the number of ounces by 30.)

1 oz	=	¹⁄₁₆ lb	=		30 g
4 oz	=	¼ lb	=		120 g
8 oz	=	½ lb	=		240 g
12 oz	=	¾ lb	=		360 g
16 oz	=	1 lb	=		480 g

Useful Equivalents for Length
(To convert inches to centimeters, multiply the number of inches by 2.5.)

1 in	=				2.5 cm
6 in	=	½ ft	=		15 cm
12 in	=	1 ft	=		30 cm
36 in	=	3 ft	= 1 yd	=	90 cm
40 in	=				100 cm =1m

Credits

Recipe Credits **Page 62; 99:** Recipes/photos: Chicken Spaghetti (pp. 130-1/131), Comfort Meatballs (pp. 172-3/172) from *The Pioneer Woman Cooks* by Ree Drummond. Copyright © 2009 by Ree Drummond. Reprinted by permission of HarperCollins Publishers. **Pages 82–83:** Chicken Pot Pie from *The Foster's Market Cookbook: Favorite Recipes for Morning, Noon and Night* by Sara Foster, copyright © 2002 by Sara Foster. Used by permission of Random House, Inc. Any third party use of this material, outside of this publication, is prohibited. Interested parties must apply directly to Random House, Inc. for permission. **Page 30; 127; 140; 148–149:** Deviled Eggs with Smoked Trout; Leek & Potato Gratin; Lemon Pudding Cake; and Sour Cream–Sweet Potato Pie from *The Beekman 1802 Heirloom Cookbook* © 2011 by Brent Ridge, Josh Kilmer-Purcell, and Sandy Gluck. Reprinted with permission from Sterling Publishing Company, Inc. **Page 61; 69; 75:** Linguine with White Clam Sauce & Coriander; Halibut with Ginger-Raisin Crust; and Pink Salmon Cakes with Dill & Mustard from *For Cod And Country* © 2011 by Barton Seaver. Reprinted with permission from Sterling Publishing Company, Inc. **Page 94; 103:** Hungarian Veal and Five-Spice Beef Stew, © 2013. Reprinted by permission of the author. **Page 56:** *Pappardelle with Escarole* recipe taken from *Nigella Express: Good Food Fast* by Nigella Lawson. Published by Chatto & Windus. Reprinted by permission of The Random House Group Limited. **Page 56:** Pappardelle with Escarole from the book *Nigella Express: Good Food Fast* by Nigella Lawson. © 2007 Nigella Lawson. Reprinted in the United States by permission of Hyperion. All rights reserved. **Page 39:** Winter Salad with Pears, Aged Cheddar, & Almonds and Apple Bread Pudding from the book *The Chew: Food. Life. Fun.* by The Chew with Contributions from Mario Batali; Gordon Elliott; Carla Hall; Clinton Kelly; Daphne Oz and Michael Symon. Copyright © 2012 Hyperion/ABC. Reprinted by permission of Hyperion. All rights reserved. **Page 141/43:** Mixed-Berry Crumble with Honey-Vanilla Ice Cream Copyright © 2009 by Ted Allen. **Page 128:** "Black-Eyed Basmati Salad" from *Guy Fieri Food* by Guy Fieri with Ann Volkwein. Copyright © 2011 by Guy Fieri. Reprinted with permission of HarperCollins Publishers. Four recipes/photos* from *Farm to Fork: Cooking Local, Cooking Fresh* by Emeril Lagasse. Copyright © 2010 by Emeril/MSLO Acquisition Sub, LLC. Reprinted by permission of HarperCollins Publishers. (***Page 29:** Herbed Goat Cheese Buttons. **Page 45–46:** Roasted Beet Salad with Walnut Dressing and Cheese Crisps. **Page 88:** Pan Roasted Duck Breasts with Apple Cider Reduction. **Pages 124–125:** Provencal-Style Stuffed Zucchini.) **Page 152:** Guava-Cream Cheese Pastillos reprinted with the permission of Atria Publishing Group, a Division of Simon & Schuster, Inc., from *Daisy: Morning, Noon and Night: Bringing Your Family Together with Everyday Latin Dishes* by Daisy Martinez. Copyright © 2010 by Daisy Martinez. All rights reserved. **Page 60:** "Pasta With Sardines, Bread Crumbs and Capers" From *The New York Times*, March 26 © 2010 *The New York Times*. All rights reserved. Used by permission and protected by the Copyright Laws of the United States. The printing, copying, redistribution, or retransmission of this Content without express written permission is prohibited. **Page 65:** "Pasta With Funghi Trifolati" From *The New York Times*, November 25 © 2012 *The New York Times*. All rights reserved. Used by permission and protected by the Copyright Laws of the United States. The printing, copying, redistribution, or retransmission of this Content without express written permission is prohibited. **Page 72:** "Last-Minute Sort-of Spanish Shrimp" From *The New York Times*, June 12 © 2012 *The New York Times*. All rights reserved. Used by permission and protected by the Copyright Laws of the United States. The printing, copying, redistribution, or retransmission of this Content without express written permission is prohibited. **Page 137:** "Stone Fruit Patchwork Bake" From "Another Tasty Way To Elude the Pie Crust" From *The New York Times*, July 29 © 2009 *The New York Times*. All rights reserved. Used by permission and protected by the Copyright Laws of the United States. The printing, copying, redistribution, or retransmission of this Content without express written permission is prohibited.

Photo Credits

Front Cover: Clockwise from top left: Hugo Burnand, Steven Freeman, Shane Bevel, Jonathan Pushnik, Diana DeLucia, Kate Mathis, Steven Freeman, Kate Mathis, Mark Peterson; Front Flap: Kate Mathis; Back Cover: Clockwise from top left: Con Poulos, Anson Smart, Greg Gorman, Paul Elledge, Melanie Acevedo, Kana Okada, Melanie Acevedo, Michael Weschler, Marcus Nilsson; Back Flap: John Kernick; **Page 1:** Kate Mathis; **Page 4:** Kate Mathis; **Pages 6–7:** Clockwise from bottom right: Laurie Smith, The Door, Paul Brissman, Brigitte Lacombe, Erin Patrice O'Brien/Corbis Outline, Scott Suchman, Scott Duncan; **Pages 8–9:** Clockwise from top left: Anson Smart, Paul Elledge, Stewart Cairns, Diana DeLucia; **Pages 10–11:** Clockwise from top left: Sara Essex Bradley, Jonathan Pushnik, Shane Bevel, Erin Patrice O'Brien/Corbis Outline. **Pages 12–13:** Clockwise from top left: Michael Weschler, John Lee Pictures, Ben Fink; **Pages 14–15:** Clockwise from top left: Quentin Bacon, Mike Pfike, Scott Suchman; **Pages 16–17:** Clockwise from bottom right: Steven Freeman, Anthony Tahlier, Craig Sjodin/ABC; **Pages 18–19:** Clockwise from top left: Hugo Burnand, Jill Lotenberg, Laurie Smith, Miki Duisterhof; **Pages 20–21:** Clockwise from top right: Greg Gorman, The Door, Sara Moulton archives; **Pages 22–23:** Clockwise from top left: Paul Brissman, Katie Stoops, Scott Duncan; **Pages 24–25:** Clockwise from top left: Gabriele Stabile, Brigitte Lacombe, Anthony Tieuli; **Page 26:** Kana Okada; **Page 28:** Steven Freeman; **Page 30:** Paulette Tavormina; **Page 33:** Kana Okada; **Page 34:** Miki Duisterhof; **Page 36:** Melanie Acevedo; **Page 38–39:** From left: Melanie Acevedo, Craig Sjodin/ABC; **Page 40:** Frances Janisch; **Page 43:** John Kernick; **Page 44:** Steven Freeman; **Page 49:** John Kernick; **Page 52:** Kana Okada; **Page 54:** Katie Stoops; **Pages 56–57:** From left: Hugo Burnand, Kana Okada; **Pages 58–59:** From left: Stephen Lovekin/Getty Images, Digital Vision/Getty Images; **Pages 62–63:** From left: Shane Bevel, John Kernick; **Page 64:** Adam/Stockfood Munich/Stockfood; **Page 66:** Frances Janisch; **Page 68:** Katie Stoops; **Page 71:** StockFood/FoodCollection; **Page 72:** Rita Maas; **Pages 74–75:** From left: Katie Stoops (2); **Page 77:** Kritsada; **Page 78:** John Kernick; **Page 81:** John Kernick; **Page 86:** Kana Okada; **Page 89:** Steven Freeman; **Page 90:** Maura McEvoy; **Page 92:** Kritsada; **Page 94–95:** From left: Courtesy of Sandra Lee, Maura McEvoy; **Page 96:** Melanie Acevedo; **Page 98–99:** From left: Melanie Acevedo, Courtesy of Ree Drummond; **Page 100:** Kate Mathis; **Pages 102–103:** From left: Getty Images, Courtesy of Sandra Lee; **Page 104:** John Kernick; **Page 106:** Yunhee Kim; **Page 108:** Kritsada; **Page 111:** Kate Mathis; **Page 113:** Jim Wright; **Page 114:** Con Poulos; **Page 116:** John Kernick; **Page 118:** Ellen Silverman; **Page 121:** Frances Janisch; **Pages 122–123:** From left: John Kernick, Kana Okada; **Page 125:** Steven Freeman; **Pages 126–127:** From left: Marcus Nilsson, Stewart Cairns; **Page 129:** Hector Sanchez; **Page 131:** Maura McEvoy; **Page 132:** Kate Mathis; **Page 134:** Melanie Acevedo; **Page 136:** From left: Barry Johnson, StockFood/Greatstock; **Page 139:** Kana Okada; **Page 141:** Anson Smart; **Page 142:** Anson Smart; **Page 145:** Andrew Eccles; **Page 146:** Melanie Acevedo; **Page 149:** Paulette Tavormina; **Page 151:** Hector Sanchez; **Page 153:** Andrew Eccles.

Index

Note: Page numbers in *italics* include recipe photos.

HEARST BOOKS

New York

An Imprint of Sterling Publishing
387 Park Avenue South
New York, NY 10016

Credits on pages 155–156

Every effort has been made to ensure that all the information in this book is
accurate. However, due to differing conditions, tools, and individual skills,
the publisher cannot be responsible for any injuries, losses, and/or other
damages that may result from the use of the information in this book.

ISBN 978-1-61837-112-6

Distributed in Canada by Sterling Publishing
c/o Canadian Manda Group, 165 Dufferin Street
Toronto, Ontario, Canada M6K 3H6
Distributed in the United Kingdom by GMC Distribution Services
Castle Place, 166 High Street, Lewes, East Sussex, England BN7 1XU
Distributed in Australia by Capricorn Link (Australia) Pty. Ltd.
P.O. Box 704, Windsor, NSW 2756, Australia

For information about custom editions, special sales, and premium and
corporate purchases, please contact Sterling Special Sales at 800-805-5489
or specialsales@sterlingpublishing.com.

Manufactured in China

2 4 6 8 10 9 7 5 3 1

www.sterlingpublishing.com